OVERCOMING DEPRESSION

Lincolnshire
COUNTY COUNCIL©

COMMUNITIES, CULTURAL SERVICES
and ADULT EDUCATION
**This book should be returned on or before
the last date shown below.**

MB)

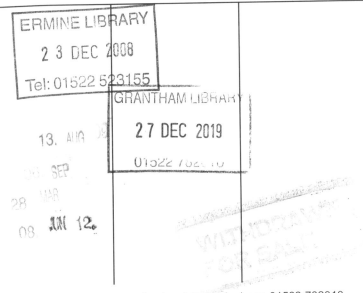

ERMINE LIBRARY

2 3 DEC 2008

Tel: 01522 523155

GRANTHAM LIBRARY

2 7 DEC 2019

01522 702 10

13. AUG

SEP

28 MAR

08 JUN 12

'19

D0860696

Overcoming Common Problems Series

A full list of titles is available from Sheldon Press,
1 Marylebone Road, London NW1 4DU, and on our website at
www.sheldonpress.co.uk

Overcoming Common Problems Series

Overcoming Common Problems Series

Overcoming Common Problems

Overcoming Depression

Dr Windy Dryden and Sarah Opie

First published in Great Britain in 2003 by
Sheldon Press
1 Marylebone Road
London NW1 4DU

British Library Cataloguing-in-Publication Data
A catalogue record for this book is available from the British Library

ISBN 0–85969–818–1

1 3 5 7 9 10 8 6 4 2

Typeset by Deltatype Ltd, Birkenhead, Wirral
Printed in Great Britain by Biddles Ltd
www.biddles.co.uk

Contents

Thank you, Andy

s.o.

1

What is Depression?

Introduction

Depression is a common problem but it is frequently misunderstood. Depression is in fact an umbrella term for a group of discrete emotional problems that have similar core symptoms. In this first chapter we will describe some of the different types of depression as well as providing some information about help that is available.

How common is depression?

At any one time approximately 5 per cent of the population meet the criteria for depression. This is likely to be a modest figure as there may be members of the depressed population who have not revealed that they are depressed. Unfortunately the number of people with depression is on the increase. Research has found that some people are more at risk of developing depression, and a number of important factors have been discovered. One factor is that depressed people can have an imbalance of chemicals in the brain. These chemicals are known as neurotransmitters, and the action of anti-depressant medication is to rebalance them. The cause of the imbalance is not certain though some contributors may be genetics, upbringing, severe loss during childhood, disruption in the sleep/wake cycle, and chronic low self-esteem. For this reason it is important that you contact your GP.

Certain groups in society appear to be more vulnerable to depression. If members of your family have been depressed then you are twice as likely to be depressed than if none were depressed. This may be because of genetic make-up (though no one has found the gene responsible) or it may be a result of environmental factors such as stressful life events. Women are twice as likely to suffer from depression as men, though this figure may be misleading as in some cultures this may be the result of the fact that men tend to hide their depression. For example, rather than classical symptoms of depression men may be more likely to show their depression through alcoholism, substance abuse and anti-social behaviour.

Types of depression

Depression was identified as a separate entity from other psychiatric disorders in the late nineteenth century, and after the Second World War different types of depression were classified (largely because of increased access to health care). The development of treatments in the 1950s meant that more research was conducted into depression and into the biological, psychological and sociological aspects that influence depression. On closer examination it was found that depression was not one condition but a group of problems. The latest edition of the *Diagnostic and Statistical Manual* for psychiatric disorders (DSM-IV) cites over 20 discrete manifestations of depression. This is significant, as treatment can vary depending on the type of depression and it may be necessary to seek advice as to the type of help that you need. The basics of some of the common types of depression are introduced in this book but it should not be used as an alternative to professional advice.

Sadness and grief

Sadness and grief are a natural reaction to a life event involving loss or change. This condition is described as normal because ordinarily the person adjusts and recovers after a period of mourning. The recovery time is influenced by the severity of the loss. There may be some temporary physical changes to sleep patterns and appetite. There may also be some changes in thinking patterns. For example, it is not uncommon after a bereavement to have obsessive thoughts about the lost person. However, those who are experiencing sadness and grief are able to see both positive and negative aspects of their lives; they are able to seek help and can look to the future with some hope.

Adjustment disorder

Adjustment disorder accompanied by a depressed mood occurs because life changes and the adjustments to these changes can be difficult. Instead of being able to see both positive and negative

2

aspects to life, you see predominantly negative. In addition, there is less hope in the future and you feel less able to ask for help or express your feelings with the appropriate people. Learning new and helpful ways of thinking and behaving can help you adjust to the change. You may not need help from a doctor to tackle the adjustment disorder. However, if your mood has deteriorated without any life change, if your emotional reaction seems overwhelming and is having a big impact on your life, then you do need to contact your GP.

Dysthymia

This is the term used to describe a chronically depressed mood with the symptoms of major depressive disorder (see next section) but less severe. Dysthymia may or may not have a triggering life event, and as such it can be confusing and frustrating for both the depressed person and their loved ones.

Major depression

Major depression is serious because it can lead to despair and hopelessness that result in people losing interest in life, being incapable of experiencing pleasure, isolating themselves and failing to look after themselves. According to DSM-IV, major depression involves at least two weeks of low mood and/or marked loss of pleasure with at least four of the following symptoms:

- sleep problems: insomnia or sleeping all the time;
- appetite problems: loss of appetite or major weight gain;
- lack of energy: apathy, lethargy, no interest in anything;
- feelings of worthlessness, hopelessness and/or terrible guilt;
- difficulty concentrating or unusual indecisiveness;
- suicidal thoughts or suicide attempts.

The key risk in the case of major depression is suicide: within five years of suffering a major depressive episode approximately a quarter of sufferers will try to kill themselves. Some people make known their intention to kill themselves, so it is important to take any talk of suicide seriously. It is important that you seek professional help from your doctor if you believe that you or a loved one may have a major depressive disorder.

Bi-polar disorder or manic depression

This affects about 1 per cent of the population. It is characterized by periods of depression, contrasted with periods of mania (high energy and unrealistic wild activity). Typically there are no clear triggers and treatment of the condition should be under the supervision of a psychiatrist.

Atypical depression

Atypical depression refers to unusual presentations of depression: for example, a person with atypical depression may appear deeply depressed, then fine for a few days, then anxious or irritable. As with other forms of depression there may be no obvious trigger to the depression.

Seasonal affective disorder (SAD)

This is a reaction to lack of sunlight. Typically, mild or major depression starts in the autumn and finishes in the spring months. The incidence of SAD increases in line with the distance from the equator. Special types of lights have been developed for the treatment of SAD.

Post-natal depression (PND)

PND is a condition that occurs after childbirth because of the hormonal changes effected by delivery and the challenges of dealing with a new baby. Two-thirds of women experience temporary sadness, 10–15 per cent become clinically depressed and about one woman in a hundred becomes so severely depressed that she needs to be hospitalized for her own safety and the safety of her babies.

The different types of depression don't always have clear boundaries and it requires professional judgement to know where, for example, a normal grief reaction may stop and a severe depression begins, so if in doubt contact your doctor. There are, however, some core symptoms of depression and these are: sadness, loss of interest, poor appetite, sleep difficulty, pessimism or guilt, and suicidal thoughts. If these symptoms have been persistent for a two-week period, then you need to see your doctor.

What this book can and cannot help

The aim of this book is to present a method of dealing with depression in terms of tackling those aspects you can influence, particularly your behaviour and your thoughts. This approach is called Rational Emotive Behaviour Therapy and will be described in more detail later. Part of dealing with depression can be to accept that there are aspects with which you may need help and then to seek out that help. Researchers into depression have found that influencing one's behaviours and thoughts can be helpful but that, with certain types of depression, this approach may not be enough: sometimes medication is necessary in combination to help lift the mood enough to reach a point where you can engage in therapy. Some types of depression are best treated medically. As a result this book will not be dealing with manic depression, severe depression, seasonal affective disorder or post-natal depression.

Who can help?

The aim of this book is to help you overcome depression. An initial step for anyone who thinks they may be depressed is to recognize when you need the help of a professional. There are a number of different services available to help you deal with depression. Often the first port of call is your GP. He or she can help you manage your depression by offering support and assessing what type of treatment is best for you. They may prescribe you some anti-depressant medication, they may suggest you have a course of talking therapy or they may decide you need to have time away from work or even some time in hospital. Your GP may recommend that you consult someone who specializes in mental health and refer you to a psychiatrist. Indeed, in some cases of depression, especially where it is severe, the involvement of a psychiatrist may well be necessary.

Other professionals allied to psychiatrists and GPs who may be involved are psychiatric nurses, occupational therapists and social workers, who can all play a vital role in helping you to deal with depression.

Clinical and counselling psychologists can provide psychological therapy for depression, as can counsellors and psychotherapists. There are many different approaches to counselling and therapy.

This book adopts a psychological approach to dealing with depression known as Rational Emotive Behaviour Therapy (REBT), which involves identifying the connection between thoughts, feelings and behaviours and learning and practising techniques that help you change those thoughts and behaviours that can contribute to or maintain your depression. Access to therapists can be gained by a referral from a professional, typically a GP or psychiatrist who considers that therapy can be beneficial to you. Alternatively, you can seek out a private therapist. If you want to take this route then there are professional bodies that have a register of therapists who have completed a required level of training and experience. You may also wish to contact self-help and voluntary organizations (such as MIND or the Depression Alliance) for support.

Seven cases of depression

In order to demonstrate an REBT approach of dealing with depression we will introduce seven fictitious people based on different presentations of depression. As you work through the book you will see how they used REBT to understand and deal with their depression and other associated problems.

Maxine

Maxine was a dedicated student. She had consistently gained A grades in her exams and coursework. Her teachers were encouraging and her parents were proud that their daughter showed such academic promise. As far as Maxine was concerned she made her family happy with her achievements and she worked hard to maintain these high standards. She had a few close friends with whom she studied. She did not socialize as much as the other students in her year as this would take valuable time away from her studies. Her family was concerned that she did not have any interests outside her schooling but concluded that their daughter was happier with her head in a book.

In her sixth-form year she sat her Cambridge University entrance exams to read medicine and was offered a place. This was a special day for Maxine and her family; it was the first time that anyone from the family had been given the opportunity to study at Cambridge.

To all intents and purposes it appeared that Maxine had a bright future ahead of her. In her final year she sat her mock examinations and her preparation was a strategic operation. She had collected previous papers and had decided to revise thoroughly a number of modules from the course that she thought would crop up in the examinations. The day of the first exam arrived and Maxine felt confident: after all, she had worked hard and had always done well before. She sat her biology and physics papers with no apparent problems, but when she read through the chemistry questions she realized that those she had revised for were not on the paper. She completed the paper as best she could and had a few nerve-racking weeks while waiting for the results.

The day of the results arrived and each student in turn was asked to see the head of the sixth form, Maxine sat down with her teacher to discuss her results. She was shocked to realize that the mistake in her revision strategy had cost her a grade. Instead of the three As she had been expecting, she received two As and a B. She did not notice the A grade results, only the B. As she discussed the exam with her teacher she could not understand why he praised her on her results. *I have failed*, she thought.

As she considered her results she questioned her abilities; the more she thought, the worse she felt, and eventually she concluded that rather than being a success she was in fact a failure. The weeks went by and Maxine continued to ruminate. She stopped studying because she anticipated that she would not succeed. In her eyes she had lost everything: she had invested so much in her studies and her academic success had been her identity. It formed the basis of her few friendships and was the source of praise from her family.

Her family were confused: they viewed her results as excellent, as did her teachers, but no matter how much they reassured Maxine that she had done well she remained convinced that she was destined to fail. She thought that the reassurance was well meaning but that if they understood properly they would agree that she was a failure.

Brian

Brian worked as a bank manager in a small town. He was good at his job and took pride in his work. He had kept himself up to date with developments and ran a very successful branch. He had enjoyed the respect of the local community that went with his status and abilities; he had been invited to stand on local committees and considered himself to be a useful member of his community. He had been married for 35 years and had two grown-up daughters who had left home and now had their own careers. Brian had spent his life dedicating himself to his career, his family and his local community.

Five years ago he was offered the opportunity to retire with a good pension but had decided against it. He now faced mandatory retirement. As the retirement date drew closer Brian's wife began to worry. She noticed that he was not his usual self. He had been having problems with his sleep: one night she had woken up at 4 a.m. to find that Brian had got up and had been sitting in the dark downstairs looking through old photographs. He had lost his appetite and, although not drinking excessively, he had uncharacteristically increased the amount of alcohol he drank.

He continued to work and put on a brave face, but his thoughts were preoccupied with what he would do after he retired. He imagined himself spending day after day with nothing of value to do, losing the respect of his community and, worst of all, relying on his family. When he thought about his future he felt more depressed and his family's attempts to support him only made matters worse.

Brian's wife tried to talk to him about his change in mood but he refused to open up about it. After weeks of her persevering he agreed to go and see his local GP. The doctor asked him a number of questions and then suggested that he might be depressed and offered him a course of anti-depressants. Brian was surprised; he had never been depressed before – he had thought that people who were depressed were simply being weak and that they would feel better if they stopped feeling sorry for themselves. With some reluctance he agreed to take the anti-depressants and to have an appointment in two weeks to review whether they were working. Brian told no one about the prescription he had been given.

Chris

As far back as he could remember, Chris had had problems forming close and lasting relationships. He had a difficult time growing up. He was an only child and did not see much of his parents. When he did see them he tried to gain their attention, but with little effect. He was regularly handed over to his grandmother and this became more frequent when his parents divorced. Despite getting on well with his grandmother he believed that his parents had rejected him. As a child he would wonder why his parents did not want him around. He would look with envy at the other children after school being met by their parents. Chris concluded that there must be something wrong with him. He maintained this thought in his adult years and as a result he formed few friends, preferring to keep himself to himself.

In his late twenties he was asked by his employers to work with a colleague on a project. He was nervous initially but after some weeks of working he gradually felt more confident. When the project ended he decided that he would take the plunge and ask his colleague out for a date. To his surprise she agreed and they went on a few dates together. Chris wondered why she accepted his invitation and why she continued to see him – surely she could do better! He found dating difficult and requested reassurance from his girlfriend that she was interested in him and would not leave. Initially this did not present a problem, but as he continued to ask for reassurance his girlfriend noticed that her reassurance did not work and he continued to express his insecurities.

Chris kept worrying that she would meet other more worthy people and would leave him. Sure enough, after a few months his girlfriend ended the relationship, saying she had found his insecurities difficult to deal with. Chris felt depressed: as far as he was concerned this was confirmation of his belief that he was unlovable and he decided that he would never risk rejection again. He turned down invitations to go out and isolated himself. After a while people stopped inviting him and he used this as further confirmation that he was not a likeable or lovable person.

Neelam

Neelam had always had a keen interest in the welfare of others. She gave regularly to a variety of charities and kept up to date with current affairs. She concerned herself with the environment, national and international injustices and inequalities in health. Every time she watched the news she thought about how she wanted to do more to help, and after speaking with a friend she found out that a local organization for homeless people was looking for volunteers.

9

After contacting the organizers she decided to go and work in the local soup kitchen. Although initially finding the work rewarding she wanted to do more, and instead of believing her efforts to be of use she considered them to be insignificant. She saw others' misfortunes as being unfair and the world as a cruel place. Neelam found that after working in the soup kitchen she had difficulty returning to her home, which was comfortable by comparison. She felt depressed when she ate food, so she ate much less. When she was not at work she thought about the plight of homeless people and spent increasing amounts of time thinking about the world's injustices. When she listened to the news on the radio or read about it in the papers, instead of regarding it as informative she found herself becoming increasingly disturbed about the troubles of the world and, as a consequence, felt more and more depressed.

Her depression was such that she had problems motivating herself and on a few occasions did not make it to the soup kitchen. She turned down invitations from friends because she thought it would be unfair for her to enjoy herself while there was so much misfortune in the world. Her depressed mood persisted, and before long she stopped her charity work altogether.

Sylvia

Sylvia was in her late fifties and lived with her husband in the suburbs. She had spent the majority of her adult years taking care of her husband and children. For Sylvia this had been a full-time job and one in which she took a great deal of pride. She had raised three children and had been both proud and sad to see them leave home to find their own way in the world. Her youngest son had just left home to move into his own flat in a neighbouring town. Sylvia was upset to see her son leave, but this time her sadness took on a different quality.

Sylvia could not shake off the thought that she was no longer useful and that she was not needed. With fewer people in the house there was less to do. Her sons and daughter were getting on with their own lives. She thought about how they had relied on her to take care of them, and at times she hoped that they would return home saying they couldn't manage without her. It was difficult to reconcile her satisfaction that she had raised three healthy, happy people with

10

the thought that in the process she had (as far as she was concerned) rendered herself useless. Her husband appeared to manage without her: because of the nature of his work he was away a great deal.

Sylvia became increasingly lonely and depressed. She had invested all her time and effort into her family and as such she didn't have a social group or hobby. She spent day after day at home alone reminiscing about the past, and when she thought about the future she believed that she would be of no use to anyone. As far as she was concerned the best years of her life had gone and life would never be the same again.

As her mood deteriorated she found that she had less energy. On some days even making herself a cup of tea or washing her hair seemed to be an enormous strain. Gradually she stopped doing things, and the less she did the less she felt like doing. Sylvia realized she was not helping herself, but her motivation had always been her family's welfare. Without this she had lost her motivation.

Lily

Lily was 17 and in her second year at ballet school. She had developed a love of dancing from an early age. At three she attended ballet classes in the village where she lived. Her teacher recognized her talent, and by the age of six Lily was taking the leading roles in productions and had begun to enter competitions, which she invariably won. Lily's parents were proud of their daughter and no expense was spared to provide her with the best facilities to encourage her talent. Her mother also invested a great deal of time in her daughter; weekends and evenings were usually dedicated to Lily's dancing activities. She won a place at ballet school and started her first term at 16, eager that her talents be recognized by a wider audience.

The school accepted students from all over the country who had demonstrated their dancing abilities, and Lily was no longer the most talented dancer in her classes. Despite working hard to improve her technique her ability remained inferior to some of her peers. At the end of the year the school staged a production and Lily hoped for a significant part. To improve her chance of being cast in a lead part she increased her efforts in class and spent hours working on her style and technique between classes.

Unfortunately, despite her efforts, Lily was offered a part in the chorus. She felt that she had been treated unfairly by her dance teacher, who knew how much effort she had put into her dancing. She felt sorry for herself and told herself how terrible it was to be treated so unfairly. Lily disturbed herself with her thoughts that life should be fair, and it was not long before she was skipping her dance classes, choosing to stay in her room and avoid her teacher and the other students.

Colin

Colin was a single man in his late fifties who had previously suffered from two spells of clinical depression. He was supported by his GP and occasionally received the help of a psychiatrist. Unfortunately, when Colin started to feel the familiar symptoms of depression he reacted by avoiding any sort of activity: he stopped washing, didn't shave and stopped his morning walk to buy the paper, so he didn't read. He couldn't be bothered to cook so he ate less. He slept badly at night so he started to sleep during the day. He felt that he was unable to change his mood, but also told himself that he must control and eradicate his depression. He concluded that he had not done so because he was a weak man, incapable of helping himself. As a result of berating himself in this way Colin was depressed about being depressed.

Summary

In this chapter we have discussed the frequency and some of the different types of depression. We have also introduced you to some of the professionals who can be of help and emphasized the importance of talking to your doctor if you are depressed. Finally we introduced you to Maxine, Brian, Chris, Neelam, Sylvia, Lily and Colin, who will help illustrate some of the strategies you can use to manage your depression. In the next chapter we will show you a method of assessing your thoughts and behaviours.

2

Using the ABC Model to Assess Depression and Sadness

Introduction

Albert Ellis originally developed Rational Emotive Behaviour Therapy (REBT) in the mid 1950s while working as a psychotherapist in New York. Ellis proposed an ABC model of emotional disturbance. This incorporates the general principle of emotional responsibility, i.e. that you largely determine your emotions by your beliefs about the situation you are in. We use the word 'largely' here partly because negative events *influence* your emotions but do not determine whether your emotional reaction is healthy or unhealthy. What determines whether your emotion is healthy or unhealthy is your belief. The good news is that if your depression is largely a result of your beliefs about a situation then you can deal with your depression by altering your beliefs. In this chapter we will introduce you to the ABCs of depression as an initial step to understanding and dealing with your depression.

The activating event (A)

The activating event is the most disturbing aspect of the situation that you are in. So, in order to find your activating event, ask yourself the question, 'What is the most depressing thing about this situation?' It is called the activating event because it activates your belief (B) that results in emotional and behavioural consequences (C). An activating event can be an actual event, such as losing a job, or alternatively it may be an inferred event, such as the thought, 'My boss thinks I'm incompetent.'

Let's apply this to Brian, whom we met in Chapter 1. The general situation is that Brian is facing mandatory retirement, but this is not his activating event. When he thinks about retirement the retirement in itself is not the most depressing aspect of the situation, but rather his prediction that he will lose a useful role in the community.

Situation:	Pending retirement.
Activating event (A):	I will lose my useful role in the community.

Notice that Brian's activating event is an inference. Brian's inference may not be accurate, but rather than challenge it at this stage we will assume that it is true. Doing so enables Brian to identify his beliefs accurately. This is important, as the beliefs largely determine his depression.

The beliefs (B)

REBT distinguishes between healthy and unhealthy negative emotions. Whether the negative emotion is healthy or unhealthy depends on whether the beliefs about the activating event are *rational* or *irrational*. Rational beliefs are termed as such because they are accurate, logical, flexible and helpful and result in healthy negative emotions such as sadness. Irrational beliefs are inaccurate, illogical, inflexible and unhelpful and result in unhealthy negative emotions such as depression.

REBT has identified the following four different irrational beliefs that result in unhealthy negative emotions.

Irrational beliefs

- *Demanding beliefs*   These tend to be expressed in words such as 'must' or 'absolutely should'. REBT proposes that of the four irrational beliefs the demand is the primary irrational belief from which the other irrational beliefs (to be discussed below) are derived.

   When Brian assessed his demanding belief about his inference that he would lose his useful role in the community it was: *I absolutely must not lose my useful role in the community.*

- *Awfulizing beliefs*   These stem from demanding beliefs. This type of belief is an extreme negative rating of the situation. Awfulizing beliefs tend to be expressed in words like 'awful', 'terrible', 'end of the world'. When you use an awfulizing belief, the implicit meaning is that the situation cannot get any worse, that it is more than 100 per cent bad and absolutely should not be

14

as bad as it is, and that no good can come out of it. So, applying this to Brian, his awfulizing belief was: *To lose my useful role in the community would be the worst thing that could happen to me.*

- *Low frustration tolerance (LFT) beliefs* These mean that you believe you cannot tolerate a situation rather than believing that it is difficult to tolerate. 'I can't stand it' or 'I can't bear it' are examples of low frustration tolerance beliefs. This points to two things: either you will die as a result of the activating event, or you will forfeit all future happiness. In Brian's case, when he thought about losing his useful role his LFT belief was: *I will not be able to tolerate losing my useful role in the community.*

- *Self/other depreciation beliefs* These are negative global ratings of oneself or someone else, based on a single or a few traits. They may also be negative global ratings of life conditions or the world. When Brian predicted that he would lose a useful role, his self-depreciation belief was: *If I lose my useful role this will prove that I am useless.*

In summary, Brian's ABC is:

Situation:	Pending retirement.
A:	I will lose my useful role in the community.
B:	I must not lose my useful role in the community. If I do, this would be the worst thing that could happen to me. I could not tolerate the loss. It would prove that I am totally useless.
C:	Depression.

Rational belief alternatives

The four irrational beliefs have rational belief alternatives that result in healthy negative emotions, in this case sadness. Why sadness is the healthy negative emotion will be explained later in the chapter.

- *Preference beliefs* These are the healthy alternative to demands. They express what you want or don't want and are realistic, flexible and logical evaluations of the situation you are in. For example, a preference belief for Brian could be: *I don't want to lose my useful role in the community but there is no universal law that states that this must not happen.* This belief demonstrates a wish to maintain a useful role but at the same time realistically acknowledges that it is not guaranteed.

- *Anti-awfulizing beliefs* These are the rational alternative to awfulizing beliefs. When your preference is not met, it is rational to conclude that the resultant situation is bad. It is also rational to conclude that this is not the worst thing that can happen, which in turn can be helpful when attempting to adapt to the situation. Anti-awfulizing beliefs give a negative rating, but the rating is within the realistic scale of 1–99.9 per cent. If Brian were to adopt an anti-awfulizing belief about his activating event he might think, *Losing my useful role in the community is pretty bad but if I put this in perspective it is far from being the worst thing that could happen to me.*

- *High frustration tolerance (HFT) beliefs* These are the rational alternative to low frustration tolerance beliefs. When your preference is not met it is rational to conclude that this is difficult to tolerate. This does not mean that you will die as a result of the activating event or that you will forfeit all future happiness. An HFT belief for Brian might be: *It would be hard for me to tolerate losing my useful role in the community, but it would be tolerable and worth tolerating because it would help me adjust to my retirement and focus on developing other interests.*

- *Self/other acceptance beliefs* These are the rational alternative to self/other depreciation beliefs. When your preference is not met, self/other acceptance beliefs enable you to say that if the block is you or another person, this can be attributed to an aspect of you or the other person. The acceptance belief acknowledges that you (or another person) are a fallible human being and cannot legitimately be defined by one or a few traits. If, on the other hand, the block is due to life conditions/the world, then acceptance beliefs enable you to be specific about the block to your preference without generalizing to all your life conditions. If we apply this principle to Brian, then his self-accepting belief would be: *If I were to lose my useful role in the community then this would not render me totally useless. It would be proof that I am a fallible human being who can reach the age of retirement. There is more to me than my work and I cannot legitimately rate my total worth as a person on whether I am retired or not.*

In summary, if Brian evaluated the activating event of losing a useful role to the community using rational beliefs his ABC would be:

Situation: Pending retirement.

A: I will lose my useful role in the community.

B: I don't want to lose my useful role in the community but there is no universal law that states that this must not happen. If it happens then that would be bad, but if I put this into perspective it is not the worst thing that could happen to me. I would find it difficult to tolerate but I could tolerate it, and tolerating it would help me adjust to my retirement and focus on developing other interests. When I lose this role I will not then become totally useless. There is more to me than my work and I cannot legitimately rate myself totally on whether I am retired or not.

C: Sadness.

The consequences (C)

As discussed, the consequences of holding beliefs about the activating event can be healthy or unhealthy. The consequences are termed healthy when they encourage people to change what can be changed and adjust to what cannot be changed. On the other hand, unhealthy consequences are those that discourage people from changing what can be changed or adjusting to what cannot be changed. REBT identifies depression as an unhealthy negative emotion and sadness as a healthy negative emotion. The important aspect is the meaning of the word you use in terms of your behaviour or how you want to behave (actions and action tendencies) and what your thoughts are like when you experience the emotion (thinking consequences).

An important issue to point out is that you can experience mild depression and this would still be unhealthy. Strong sadness, on the other hand, would be healthy. It is not the intensity of the mood that results in it being healthy or unhealthy but the action tendencies and thinking consequences. For the purposes of this book, when we talk about sadness we refer to a healthy emotion in response to loss or failure as a result of rational beliefs. The *thinking consequences* of sadness are:

- the ability to see both the negative and positive aspects of failure;
- less likelihood of thinking of other losses and failures than when depressed;
- the ability to seek help;
- the ability to look to the future with hope.

The *action tendencies* of sadness are:

- to express feelings about loss or failure and to talk about these feelings to significant people;
- to seek out reinforcements after a period of mourning.

When we refer to depression we are talking about an unhealthy negative emotion in response to loss or failure as a result of irrational beliefs. The *thinking consequences* of depression are:

- only seeing the negative aspects of loss or failure;
- thinking of other losses and failures that one has experienced;
- thinking one is unable to help oneself (helplessness);
- only seeing pain and bleakness in the future (hopelessness).

The *action tendencies* of depression are:

- to withdraw from reinforcements;
- to withdraw into oneself;
- to create an environment consistent with depressed feelings;
- to attempt to terminate feelings of depression in self-destructive ways.

When we apply the above criteria to Brian we can see that he is depressed rather than sad, because his thinking consequences are that he sees only the negative aspects of the loss of his role and only pain and bleakness in the future. In addition, his behaviour has become depressed in that he has withdrawn from reinforcements such as family support; he has withdrawn into himself by not communicating his feelings; and he is dealing with his depression in self-destructive ways by increasing his alcohol intake.

Problems and goals

The criteria for depression and sadness identify emotional, behavioural (and thinking) consequences. Thus, when learning how to deal with your depression, you can have emotional, behavioural (and thinking) goals. The benefit of having behavioural as well as emotional goals is that you can monitor your progress towards the emotional goal of sadness. Let us look again at Brian and consider his identified problems and goals.

- *Emotional problem:* depression about losing his useful role in the community. The depression is a block to Brian making adjustments for his pending retirement.
- *Behavioural problem:* (1) I have withdrawn from my family; (2) I have refused to talk with the appropriate people about my feelings about retirement; (3) I drink alcohol to deal with my depression.

- *Emotional goal:* sadness about losing his useful role in the community. The sadness about the loss enables Brian to adjust to pending retirement and take steps towards other personal development goals.
- *Behavioural goal:* (1) to spend more time with my family; (2) to talk with my family and other appropriate people about my feelings in relation to retirement; (3) to reduce my alcohol intake and use more constructive ways to deal with my depression.

Psychological vulnerability to depression

Here we will look at some of the personal philosophies that people have that mean they are more likely to depress themselves.

Autonomy and sociotropy

So far we have discussed the ABC of depression and established that the beliefs are central in determining whether you are depressed or sad. But why do we form irrational beliefs about one thing rather

19

than another? We only disturb ourselves about those things that are important to us and we decide what is important to us through our life experiences. Dr Aaron T. Beck, a famous psychiatrist and cognitive therapist, was interested in the observation that people disturb themselves with beliefs that refer to the importance they place on particular characteristics. This has resulted in the notion of autonomy and sociotropy characteristics.

Autonomy

Autonomy-type vulnerability applies to those people who attribute a high degree of importance to autonomy. They value autonomous characteristics such as success, freedom and independence, and tend to invest their efforts to achieve these aims. Those with strong autonomy characteristics are more vulnerable to irrational beliefs that result in depression when their desires for success, mobility and independence are blocked. They may also maintain a depression by autonomy-type behaviours such as not asking for help.

Sociotropy

Sociotropy-type vulnerability refers to a person's investment in relationships with other people. They place a high degree of importance on acceptance from others, intimacy, support and guidance. This type of vulnerability means that irrational beliefs are activated when the person experiences or infers that they are misunderstood, unsupported or rejected.

They may also maintain their depression by relying on others as a support rather than by helping themselves.

Self-blame, self-pity and other pity

Dr Paul Hauck suggested that we take another look at the psychological causes of depression as he noticed that his patients had three different psychological vulnerabilities to depression.

Self-blame

This refers to the process many depressed people go through of being too critical of themselves. If you engage in a philosophy of self-blame, you may call yourself useless when you retire (as Brian does) or you may call yourself unlovable because your partner leaves you (as Chris did – see Chapter 1). Self-blame can involve sociotropy and autonomy vulnerabilities, but the most significant aspect of this philosophy is not what you disturb yourself about but that you blame yourself and hold self-deprecating beliefs.

Self-pity
The second psychological vulnerability to depression is when you feel sorry for yourself when you do not get what you want, or have a tendency to feel depressed when you think that life is not fair or that people have been unkind. Consider Lily, whom we met in Chapter 1. Lily engaged in self-pity when she went to college and found she was no longer the most talented dancer. She lost confidence in her abilities and thought that it was terribly unfair that she had put so much time and effort into her dancing only to be given a small part in the production. As in self-blame, self-pity can include both the sociotropy and autonomy domains, but in addition demanding and awfulizing beliefs are present. It can be difficult for people to accept that their depression may be a result of self-pity, but if you suspect that you may be engaging in self-pity then it is in your interests to address this vulnerability.

Other pity
Just as you can promote depression by feeling sorry for yourself, you can also promote depression by feeling sorry for others. Consider Neelam, whom we met in Chapter 1. She disturbed herself about the plight of homeless people and spent long periods thinking about the world's injustices. Rather than this encouraging her to take action, she lost motivation and was less active. Neelam is likely to promote depression in herself by her philosophy of other pity. Other pity involves both demanding beliefs, such as: *People absolutely should not experience misfortune when they don't deserve it*, and awfulizing beliefs, such as: *It is terrible that people experience misfortune when they don't deserve it.*

Common blocks to our goals

Now we have looked at the ABC of depression and some of the psychological vulnerabilities to depression, let us move on to look specifically at some of the common blocks to our goals that can occur in a lifetime. These represent activating events, and we have included the associated irrational beliefs that can cause and maintain depression.

A prescription for a depression-causing philosophy

1 *Failure*: I have to succeed in all I do. If I fail then I am a failure.
2 *Incompetence*: I must do well. If I do not then this shows that I am totally incompetent.
3 *Loss of useful role*: I have to be useful. If I am not useful then I am useless and will never be of use again.
4 *Loss of status*: I must maintain my status. My status is the be-all and end-all in my life and to lose it would make me worthless.
5 *Relying on others*: I have to be self-reliant at all times. If I were to rely on others this would show that I am a weak person.
6 *Depression*: I must not be depressed. Depression is a sign of weakness. If I am depressed then I am weak.
7 *Disapproval*: I have to be approved of at all times by all people. If I am disapproved of then this means that I am either a bad person or an unlikeable person.
8 *Loss of love*: I must be loved in my close relationships. If I am not loved then this means that I am unlovable.
9 *Criticism*: I must not be criticized. If I am criticized then there is something wrong with me as a person.
10 *Not belonging*: I must belong to my chosen social group. If my social group does not accept me then this will be terrible as I will never experience happiness.
11 *Loss of helping role*: I have to be helpful to others. If I am not helpful to others then I have no worth.
12 *Unattractiveness*: I must be attractive to look at. If I am not attractive then I am an ugly person.
13 *Others withdrawing care/support*: In order to feel OK I have to be looked after and supported by other people. I could not bear it if others withdrew their support and care for me.
14 *Unfairness to self*: Life must be fair. Unfairness is terrible and I cannot tolerate it.
15 *Others' misfortune*: People absolutely should not experience misfortune when they do not deserve it.
16 *Hardship*: Life must not be hard.

17 *Bereavement*: My loved one absolutely should not have died. I cannot put up with their death. My life has lost all meaning.
18 *Goal frustration*: I must achieve my goal without frustration. To struggle for goal attainment is intolerable.

Summary

We began this chapter by introducing you to the ABC model of depression. We then explored some of the psychological vulnerabilities to depression, and finally looked at some of the common blocks to our goals. In the next chapter we will show you how you maintain your depression and how to activate yourself.

3

Depressed Behaviour

Introduction

In Chapter 1 we described the different types of depression and in Chapter 2 we introduced you to the types of beliefs that underpin depression. In this chapter we will begin by showing you how you maintain your depression through your thoughts and behaviours, and we will then show you how to activate yourself, which is a crucial step in overcoming depression.

By the term 'maintain your depression' we mean that once depression sets in, people tend to think and act in certain self-defeating ways (see Chapter 2, pp. 17–19). This in turn promotes more irrational beliefs which lead to more depression which sparks more negative thinking and self-defeating behaviours, and the cycle goes on.

To demonstrate this, consider Sylvia, whom we met in Chapter 1. Sylvia disturbed herself when the last of her children left home. When she felt depressed she stayed at home on her own and spent her time reminiscing about the past. When she thought about the future she believed that she would be of no use to anyone. As her mood deteriorated she found she had less and less energy, and responded to this by doing less. The less she did the less she felt like doing. Sylvia lost her motivation to the point where making a cup of tea or washing her hair was an enormous effort.

The effects of inactivity

As previously discussed, inactivity is bad for depression, and we can see from Sylvia's predicament what can happen. There are a number of reasons why inactivity is going to make it more difficult for you to deal with your depression and may well make it worse. Below are some of the more common problems associated with inactivity. See if you can identify any similarities with your behaviour in response to feeling depressed.

Inactivity gives you time and space to disturb yourself

A problem with inactivity is that it gives you plenty of time to disturb yourself. Think about how you feel when you are inactive, particularly if you are on your own. For many depressed people this is time to think about the situations that activate irrational beliefs and thus lead to more depression. The more you rehearse your irrational beliefs and tell yourself, for example, that you are useless or that the world is a terrible place, the worse you feel. For people who are depressed, inactivity is often a solitary exercise; as such, there is no one to contradict your irrational beliefs so they remain in place, unchallenged. Consider Sylvia again. She reduced her activity, stayed at home and spent her time reminiscing about the past. This provided her with hours of time dedicated to thinking about losing her family and her role within the family. Her inactivity meant that there were no distractions and thus she focused almost entirely on her irrational self-deprecating belief that she was useless. As irrational beliefs largely determine depression, Sylvia's depression grew worse.

Inactivity reinforces irrational beliefs

Through her inactivity, Sylvia denied herself the chance to demonstrate that she could be useful. The evidence she had was that she was useful only when she took care of her family, so she reinforced her belief that (as the focus of her use had gone) she was now useless. This, of course, was not true, but it was difficult for Sylvia to see things otherwise while she was inactive.

Chris had a similar dilemma. He believed himself to be unlovable and this interfered with his ability to form relationships. After an attempt at a relationship, where he continually asked for reassurance, his girlfriend left him. He used the experience as confirmation that he was indeed unlovable. Following this he decided that he would never risk rejection again and he turned down invitations and isolated himself. After a while people stopped inviting him and Chris used this as further confirmation of his unlovability.

This is another example of how inactivity (this time in the form of social withdrawal) reinforces a person's irrational beliefs. It would be difficult for Chris to change his irrational belief that he was unlovable without any social contact. So he effectively reinforced his belief through his actions. You may have noticed that Chris had a self-depreciating belief where he considered himself to be unlovable; this suggests a sociotropy-type vulnerability to depression. By avoiding social contact he guaranteed that he would not experience intimacy, acceptance and sharing qualities, valued by those with sociotropy leanings. Thus, through his inactivity he denied himself the human experience he valued the most.

Inactivity reduces motivation

Have you ever noticed that the less you do the less you feel like doing? This is the effect of inactivity on motivation. It is sometimes referred to as the lethargy cycle. Take Colin from Chapter 1. He had been depressed on two previous occasions and reacted to his depression by avoiding activity. This episode of depression was no different; he stopped washing regularly and didn't shave. He stopped his morning walk with the dog to buy the paper, and so didn't read. He ate less because he didn't make food for himself, and he spent his afternoons asleep. Colin changed his activity level because he felt depressed and one of his symptoms was lethargy. His body felt heavier and when he walked he felt as though he had weights tied to his feet – in fact, all physical movement was more difficult. In response to this he reduced his activity level and did not start any activity again until his depression went. He was waiting to feel better. The problem with this stance was that he ended up experiencing depression for longer than if he had been more active.

We have already seen how inactivity gives you extra time to disturb yourself and how inactivity reinforces your irrational beliefs. However, in addition to this, low motivation and inactivity can be both a symptom of depression and a trigger for further depression. If you are depressed and wait to feel motivated before you get active, then you will wait a long time. In actual fact, activity comes before motivation, so you can break the lethargy cycle by *gradually* increasing the amount of activity you do when you are depressed. We emphasize the word 'gradually' because some people with depression try to do too much and set themselves up to fail, thus reinforcing their belief that they are incapable. We will discuss this later in the chapter.

Inactivity reinforces helplessness

One of the reasons that Colin was inactive when depressed was because he believed that there was nothing he could do for himself to relieve his symptoms of depression. Unfortunately, the belief that you cannot help yourself is common in depression. If you refer in Chapter 1 to the diagnostic criteria for major depressive disorder, a sense of helplessness is one of the symptoms. Martin Seligman, an American psychologist, suggested that inactivity reinforces a sense of helplessness, and vice versa. For example, once you think that obtaining a desirable outcome is impossible and that you are unable to prevent an undesirable outcome occurring, then you may fail to take any action aimed at influencing your situation. Your failure to take action then reinforces the belief that you are unable to help yourself.

If we apply this to Colin, his desired outcome was an end to his depression and his undesirable outcome was that it should continue. He believed that he was unable to help himself reach his desired outcome (no depression) or prevent the undesirable outcome (of it continuing), so he didn't try to help himself. The main problem with this was that Colin's belief that he was helpless increased his conviction, which served to maintain his depression. In addition to this, he made himself more vulnerable to future episodes of depression than if he had identified what activities he could realistically engage in to facilitate his recovery and had then done them.

Inactivity reinforces hopelessness

A sense of hopelessness can be both an activating event and a thinking consequence of depression. As we have seen, Colin was inactive because he believed he was unable to help himself. In addition, he was hopeless about his future. A behavioural conse-quence of his hopelessness was inactivity. Through inactivity he maintained his depression and this resulted in increased hopelessness about the future. As with thoughts of helplessness, a vicious cycle ensues. This cycle can be broken by activity. When depressed,

Colin's thinking consequence was that the future was hopeless, and when he inferred that the future was hopeless he activated irrational beliefs resulting in more depression. For example:

A1 = I am helpless in controlling my depression.

B1 = I absolutely have to control my depression. It is terrible that I cannot control it and I am a weak man for not controlling my depression.

C1 = depression (emotion); inactivity (behaviour consequence)
   = I will always be depressed (thinking consequence reflects hopelessness).

↓

A2 = I will always be depressed.

B2 = I must see an end to my depression and it is terrible to think that I will be depressed in the future.

C2 = depression (emotional consequence); inactivity (behavioural consequence).

Colin was stuck in a cycle where his behavioural and thinking consequences would at best maintain his depression and at worst trigger beliefs that increased the severity of his depression.

Inactivity affects self-confidence

In Chapter 1 we met Maxine who was depressed when she disturbed herself about her A-level results. She believed that her results were an indication that she was a failure. The behavioural consequence of her feeling depressed was that she stopped studying, lost confidence in her abilities and so refused to risk further confirmation of her belief that she was a failure. The problem with Maxine's approach to resolving this crisis of confidence is that she in fact reinforced the belief that she was a failure through her inactivity. If you don't risk failure then, of course, you do not fail – and you also do not succeed. Maxine deprived herself of possible success and, more importantly, of learning how to cope constructively with failure. So long as she identified herself with someone who was a failure and refused to take action, she would remain vulnerable to depression.

How to break the cycle

As you can see from the experience of Sylvia, Maxine, Colin and Chris, thoughts and behaviours have a reciprocal effect on each other and you can easily maintain or even worsen your depression through your response to it. The idea that you can unwittingly maintain your depression through the behavioural consequence of inactivity has been supported by research into depression. There are numerous studies that endorse the idea that activity-based interventions are best done early on in your road to recovery. As behaviours are easier to change than thoughts and feelings, taking action first will be more likely to give you some initial success in dealing with your depression. This in turn will help you to build up confidence and facilitate the change from irrational to rational beliefs that is crucial in overcoming your depression. In fact, psychotherapists who use REBT and other cognitive approaches to psychotherapy tend to assist their depressed clients to identify and change their unhelpful behaviours as a first step and then progress to changing irrational beliefs, particularly when inactivity is a prominent feature of the client's depression.

The process of behavioural activation is based on the idea that being active leads to rewards that are an antidote to depression. One way of doing this would be to complete an activity schedule.

Activity schedules

An activity schedule is a plan for the activities that you aim to undertake. The plan is made for a day or a week at a time and includes activity that would ordinarily give you a sense of achievement or a sense of pleasure. The aims of the schedule are to establish a structure for the day; to increase your chance of experiencing a sense of achievement and a sense of pleasure; to improve your energy level and thereby to promote motivation. To show you how an activity schedule works, we will use Sylvia as an example.

Step 1: Assess your behaviour for a typical day
As we have seen, Sylvia's days were unstructured and her time was filled with thoughts and actions that maintained (and worsened) her depression. Here is an account of a typical day.

DEPRESSED BEHAVIOUR

Name...................Sylvia ....

Time	Activity
7–8	Wake up
8–9	Stay in bed but don't sleep
9–10	Stay in bed but don't sleep
10–11	Stay in bed but don't sleep
11–12	Stay in bed but don't sleep
12–1	Make myself tea and toast
1–2	Watch daytime TV (though I don't really watch it)
2–3	Watch daytime TV (though I don't really watch it)
3–4	Watch daytime TV (though I don't really watch it)
4–5	Start to feel a bit better so I shower and dress myself
5–6	Make dinner
6–7	Eat dinner
7–8	Eat dinner
8–9	Watch TV (though I don't really watch it) with my husband if he's in

9–10	Watch TV (though I don't really watch it) with my husband if he's in
10–11	Go to bed

Through the process of writing down what your typical day is like when you are depressed, it is easy to see how periods of activity and inactivity can influence your mood in the day. You may also see how mood can influence your activity level. For example, Sylvia noticed that she was most inactive when her mood was at its worst and most active when it was at its best. It is clear that she does not use activity as a coping strategy, and it is possible that through the use of activity scheduling she may be able to influence her mood (and influence her thoughts).

Step 2: Schedule activities for the day
When you write a schedule of daily activities for yourself there are a number of important points to bear in mind:

- Set realistic targets for the day; unrealistic targets will increase the likelihood that you will be unsuccessful and could reinforce your sense of failure.
- Write a schedule that includes some activities that you normally enjoy, as this will increase your chance of experiencing pleasure.
- Write a schedule that includes something that would normally give you a sense of achievement, as this will increase your chance of experiencing a sense of mastery.

Sylvia was able to identify the fact that she had most difficulty getting washed and dressed in the morning. She also realized that she used to like walks in the park and that she enjoyed gardening, and that normally after an afternoon gardening she gained a sense of achievement. Using this information, Sylvia wrote a schedule for herself.

Name...................Sylvia ....

Time	Activity
7–8	Get up and make tea
8–9	Wash and dress
9–10	Eat breakfast
10–11	Read a section of the newspaper
11–12	Walk in the park
12–1	Walk in the park
1–2	Lunch
2–3	Gardening
3–4	Gardening
4–5	Wash and change
5–6	Prepare evening meal
6–7	Eat evening meal
7–8	Phone sister
8–9	Watch TV

9–10	Bath
10–11	Bed

Step 3: Carry out the schedule

When you carry out your schedule write down next to each activity whether you completed it, using a tick, and record whether you enjoyed the activity (P = pleasure) and whether you gained a sense of achievement (M = mastery).

When Sylvia completed her schedule she noticed the effect of activity on her depression.

Name..................Sylvia.. .

Time	Activity	
7–8	Get up and make tea	✓
8–9	Get washed and dressed	✓
9–10	Eat breakfast	✓
10–11	Read a section of the newspaper	
11–12	Walk in the park	✓ P
12–1	Walk in the park	✓ P
1–2	Lunch	✓
2–3	Gardening	✓ P & M

3–4	Gardening	✓ P & M
4–5	Wash and change	✓
5–6	Prepare evening meal	✓
6–7	Eat evening meal	✓
7–8	Phone sister	✓ P
8–9	Watch TV	✓
9–10	Bath	✓
10–11	Bed	✓

Step 4: Evaluate your schedule

Once you have completed your schedule, look back over the day to see what activities were helpful in promoting a sense of mastery and pleasure. If we look at Sylvia's completed activity schedule, we see that she completed all of the activities except reading a section of the paper. She also recorded that she enjoyed her walk in the park and phoning her sister and that she gained a sense of achievement and enjoyment from her afternoon gardening. For Sylvia, the activity schedule served as an antidote to her depressed behaviour and helped to distract her from her thoughts about her family and the irrational belief that she was useless. Thus the activity schedule has helped her to manage her depression and provide some respite, but in order to deal with her depression she will also need to challenge her irrational belief that she is useless. This process will be discussed in Chapter 4, but the activity schedule has provided Sylvia with some valuable evidence that she is not totally useless which she can use when she starts to dispute her irrational beliefs.

34

Graded task assignments

Have you ever noticed that activities that you would ordinarily have no problem completing can appear impossible when you are depressed? If this is the case, dividing an activity into separate tasks can be helpful. As the term implies, graded task assignments involve grading tasks in order of difficulty so that you start with the easiest first and work your way up. Success is the completion of a task, not the completion of the entire activity, and for those people who have problems completing the task it can be broken down further.

For example, from Sylvia's activity schedule it was apparent that she did not complete the activity of reading the paper. This was because she found it difficult to concentrate and read the same two lines of the paper over and over. Rather than persevere with an activity as a complete task, one option would have been to break it down into a number of graded tasks. In general, a task can be broken down in terms of:

1 *time* (e.g. do only ten minutes' work and then stop, no matter how much or how little you have done);
2 *place* (e.g. work in only one place on that day);
3 *stages* (e.g. don't try and do every assignment in one go).

Thus Sylvia could break down her task of reading a section of the newspaper by time (e.g. reading for only five minutes and stopping) or by stages (e.g. read only five lines of the paper and then stop).

The most important thing to remember when designing a behavioural task for yourself, such as a graded task assignment or an activity schedule, is that you need to activate and challenge yourself but not overwhelm yourself. Behavioural exercises can help to combat both a sense of helplessness, by providing current evidence of your ability to help yourself, and a sense of hopelessness, by providing evidence that your depressed feelings can fluctuate and therefore improve. In addition, activity can improve your motivation and energy, thus breaking the lethargy cycle. It can provide valuable evidence that you can use it to dispute your irrational beliefs and distract you from your depressed thinking.

This final point is important, as a number of research studies have indicated that while a person is depressed their memory is impaired. This is particularly true for positive memories (though it returns to normal once depression subsides). As a result, if you try to remember positive events in your life as a way of gaining evidence that counteracts your irrational beliefs, you may find this difficult when you are depressed.

Other helpful behaviours

In addition to the above behavioural strategies designed to help you overcome your depression, there are a number of other ways you can help yourself.

Reduce your alcohol intake

Alcohol has a powerful effect on your mood, and although initially you may feel better after a drink, in the long run you will feel worse. Some people notice that their mood deteriorates greatly after consuming alcohol and so abstain from alcohol completely. Some people who misuse alcohol find that their symptoms of depression disappear once they complete their detox programmes.

Promote a healthy sleep/wake cycle

Although some sleep problems associated with depression are biochemically based, sleep disturbance can be maintained by a number of unhelpful behaviours. For example, if you have a poor night's sleep and then return to bed during the day to catch up on sleep, you will find it difficult to sleep well the following night. Another problem associated with depression is hypersomnia (too much sleep). Even though you feel tired and drained when you are depressed, you do not need any more sleep than you did before your depression started. Sleeping during the day will only serve to maintain the problem. Some tips for restoring a healthy sleep/wake cycle are:

- keep to fixed retiring and rising times;
- avoid taking naps during the day; if you need to relax, use alternative methods such as listening to music or reading;
- avoid using your bedroom for activities other than sleeping;

- remove external distractions such as noise and lights as much as possible;
- avoid stimulants such as caffeine;
- if you have worrying thoughts, write them down and aim to deal with them the next day;
- use relaxation exercises or relaxation tapes before you retire.

Maintain a healthy diet

As one of the symptoms of depression can be a reduction or increase in appetite, you may feel like eating little or you may eat too many comfort foods; in either case your diet may be poor.

A balanced diet is important for your physical health but it is also important for your mental health. For example, a diet that contains complex carbohydrates such as potatoes, pasta and wholegrain breads can raise levels of serotonin in the brain, one of the neurotransmitters that has an anti-depressant effect. In fact, people who have seasonal affective disorder experience carbohydrate craving. On the other hand, some nutritionists say that sugar can exacerbate depression (as well as anxiety, irritability and fatigue). If you are concerned about the effect of food on your depression or suspect you may have a food allergy, you may wish to consult a dietician.

Summary

In this chapter we have shown you some of the ways in which you can unwittingly maintain your depression through the way you behave, and have also described various techniques designed to help you to activate yourself. Finally, we looked at other behaviours you can control that may help you deal with symptoms of depression. While these activities are important, in isolation they may not be enough to overcome your depression. In order to do this you will need to dispute the irrational beliefs that largely determine whether, as a consequence, you experience healthy sadness or unhealthy depression. In the next chapter we will show you how to dispute your irrational beliefs and integrate rational beliefs into your belief system.

4

Challenging Your Irrational Beliefs

Introduction

In the previous chapter we discussed some of the reasons why inactivity maintains depression. We also showed you some methods to activate yourself when you are depressed, which is a crucial step in overcoming depression. In this chapter we will show you how you can challenge irrational beliefs that underpin depression and reinforce the rational beliefs that bring you closer to the emotional goal of healthy sadness.

Before you challenge your unhealthy beliefs let us remind you of the ABC of depression discussed in Chapter 2. The *activating event* (A) is the aspect of the situation you are in that you are most disturbed about. *Irrational beliefs* (IB) about the activating event (A) are illogical, irrational, inflexible and unhelpful and largely determine the *consequence* (C) of unhealthy depression. Alternatively, the same *activating event* (A) when evaluated using *rational beliefs* (RB) that are logical, rational, flexible and helpful will largely determine a *consequence* (C) of healthy sadness. As a reminder, consider Brian's ABCs which we discussed in Chapter 2.

Unhealthy ABC

A: I will lose my useful role in the community.
IB: I must not lose my useful role in the community (demand). If I do, this would be the worst thing that could happen to me (awfulizing), I could not tolerate the loss (LFT). It would prove that I am totally useless (self-depreciation).
C: Depression.

Behavioural consequences: withdrawal from my family; refusal to talk about my feelings in relation to retirement; drink alcohol to drown sorrows.

Thinking consequences: only look at the negative aspects of retirement; think the future will be bleak.

In Chapter 2 we showed you that for every irrational belief there is a rational alternative. We went on to show you Brian's rational beliefs about his pending retirement.

Healthy ABC

A: I will lose my useful role in the community.

B: I don't want to lose my useful role in the community but there is no law that states this must not happen (preference). If it happens then that would be bad, but if I put this into perspective it is not the worst thing that could happen to me (anti-awfulizing). I would find it hard to tolerate but I could tolerate it and tolerating it would help me adjust to my retirement and focus on developing other interests (HFT). When I lose this particular role I will not then become totally useless. There is more to me than my work and I cannot legitimately rate myself totally on whether I am retired or not (self-acceptance).

C: Sadness.

Behavioural consequences: spend more time with my family; talk to my family and other appropriate people about my feelings in relation to my retirement; use constructive ways to deal with sadness; develop other interests.

Thinking consequences: look at both the positive and negative aspects of retirement; think that the future looks hopeful although there may be problems ahead.

Notice that the activating event remains the same for the healthy and unhealthy ABC. The beliefs change, and they are central in determining whether the emotional consequence is unhealthy depression or healthy sadness. Now, at this stage Brian is aware that his beliefs play a central role in depression about his retirement. This is an important stage in overcoming depression using REBT, as you will use this insight to help you challenge your beliefs. If you are unsure of the central role that beliefs play in your depression and sadness then we advise you to re-read Chapter 2.

Challenging your depression-creating beliefs

The purpose of challenging beliefs is to understand why the irrational beliefs that underpin your depression are unhealthy and why the rational beliefs that underpin sadness are healthy. This is referred to as intellectual insight. This intellectual insight is an important first step in helping you overcome your depression and bringing you closer to the emotional goal of healthy sadness. Without this understanding of why your beliefs are irrational beliefs and why your rational beliefs are rational, you may fall into the trap of replacing an irrational belief with rational beliefs without conviction. Rational beliefs will only help you overcome your depression if you believe them, and the process of challenging belief is a tried and tested way of increasing your conviction.

However, challenging your irrational and rational beliefs about a specific situation is unlikely to be enough by itself to overcome your depression. In order to do this you will need to work at integrating and acting on your healthy rational beliefs. In the next chapter we will show you some of the techniques you can use to help you to integrate and act on rational beliefs. So be realistic about your expectation at this stage: your aim is to gain intellectual insight.

Arguments used to challenge your depression-creating beliefs

As we have shown, unhealthy depression-creating beliefs are irrational. If you recall from Chapter 2, irrational beliefs have a number of common characteristics. Irrational beliefs are rigidly held beliefs that are unhelpful, inconsistent with reality and illogical. These characteristics provide the basis of the following three main arguments used to challenge your depression-creating beliefs:

- *pragmatic arguments*, e.g. is this belief helpful?
- *scientific arguments*, e.g. is this belief consistent with reality?
- *logical arguments*, e.g. is this belief logical?

These questions are designed to help you to appreciate why the irrational beliefs that underpin your depression are unhealthy, i.e. to gain intellectual insight. Let's look at these arguments in more detail.

Pragmatic arguments

By using pragmatic arguments you consider the effects of holding an irrational belief compared with the effects of holding a rational belief. This can be a helpful argument as REBT spells out the behavioural and thinking consequences of holding irrational beliefs and their rational counterparts. You may wish to check the behavioural and thinking consequences of depression and sadness in Chapter 2 before using this argument on your specific ABC.

Now try asking yourself the following pragmatic questions:

- Where will it get me to believe that I . . . ?
- What are the emotional and behavioural consequences of believing that I . . . ?
- Is my belief helping me to achieve my goal?
- Is it healthy for me to believe that . . . ?
- Will my belief hinder me in the pursuit of my goal?
- What are the advantages and disadvantages of holding this belief?

Scientific arguments

When you use scientific arguments you are looking, like a scientist, for empirical evidence, and in this case it is evidence that will prove or disprove your belief. For example, consider Maxine, whom we met in Chapter 1. Maxine may challenge her irrational belief by asking: 'Where is the evidence that I am a total failure?' While there is evidence that Maxine has dropped a grade in an exam there is no evidence that she is a total failure. As discussed in earlier chapters, the REBT theory of the self is that the self is made up of all the thoughts, feelings, behaviours and characteristics that constitute a person. To be a total failure Maxine would have to have failed at everything. In addition to this she would never be able to succeed in the future. No matter how much Maxine 'feels' that she is a failure, this is clearly not the case so the belief is not true.

And consider Chris, whom we also met in Chapter 1. Using the scientific argument, Chris challenges his demanding belief, 'Is my belief that my partner has to show me affection at all times consistent with reality?' The answer here is that his demand is inconsistent with reality. While his desire to be shown affection is consistent with reality, his demand that his partner has to show

41

affection at all times is not. If his belief were true, then his partner would in fact show affection at all times, whether she wanted to or not!

Examples of scientific arguments are:

- Is there any evidence that I ... ?
- Where is the evidence that I ... ?
- Would a scientist agree that there was evidence to prove that my belief is true?
- Is my belief consistent with reality?
- Can I prove my belief is true?

Logical arguments
Logical arguments check whether your belief is correctly reasoned and consistent. By using logical argument you need to refer to the rational belief and ask yourself whether the irrational belief is a logical conclusion. So, for example, can Maxine logically conclude that because she dropped a grade in an exam she is a total failure? The answer here is no, because she cannot logically rate her whole being on the basis of a single event. Also consider Chris. Can he conclude that because he wants his partner to show him affection she absolutely has to? Again the answer here is no, because there is no logical connection. Chris starts out with a preference that he wants his partner to show him affection. This is flexible, but the conclusion that therefore she absolutely has to is inflexible. As logical thought is consistent thought, you cannot logically derive an inflexible conclusion from a flexible start.

Some questions to test the logic of your beliefs are:

- Is it logical to say that I must ... ?
- Is my belief logical?
- Is it logical to conclude that because I want ... therefore I must ... ?
- Does my 'must' follow on logically from my preference?
- Where is the logic in my belief that ... ?

Using the three major arguments with irrational beliefs

Now we have looked at the three main arguments used in Rational Emotive Behaviour Therapy, we will show you how they can be used to challenge the four irrational beliefs. As an example, we will employ the challenges to Brian's irrational and rational beliefs about his pending retirement.

Using the three major arguments with demands

You will recall from Chapter 2 that demands are rigid evaluations in the form of 'must', 'absolutely should', 'have to', 'got to'. Taking Brian's example, his demand is expressed as: *I must not lose my useful role in the community.*

- *Is this belief helpful?*
  Answer: Using the pragmatic argument, Brian's belief that he must not lose his useful role is not helpful, as the result is that he feels depressed and predicts a totally negative future.

- *Is this belief consistent with reality?*
  Answer: Using the scientific argument, Brian's demand is inconsistent with reality because his useful role in the community is that of a bank manager and there is no law of the universe decreeing that he must not retire from this role. Had his demand been consistent with reality then there would be no way that he could ever retire, even if he wanted to.

- *Is this belief logical?*
  Answer: Using the logical argument, there is no logical connection between his desire not to lose this role and his demand that he must not. His desire not to lose this role is flexible and his demand that he must not is inflexible, and as logical thought is consistent thought, you can't logically change a flexible into an inflexible.

Applying the three arguments to awfulizing

Awfulizing beliefs are extreme negative evaluations. Brian identified his awfulizing belief as: *If I lose my useful role that would be the worst thing that could happen to me.*

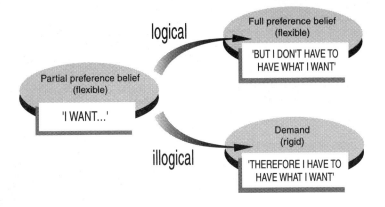

- *Is this belief helpful?*
  Answer: Clearly the answer is no, as the awfulizing belief results in his feeling depressed. While depressed Brian has unhelpful thinking consequences, in that he predicts a totally negative future. He also engages in unhealthy behaviours such as withdrawing from his family and friends and drinking more alcohol.

- *Is this belief true?*
  Answer: Brian's belief is not true, because while he can prove that he views losing his useful role in the community as negative, he cannot prove that it is the worst thing that can happen to him. In fact, he can probably prove there are far worse things that can happen to him.

- *Is this belief logical?*
  Answer: While it is bad that Brian is to lose his useful role it is not logical to conclude that it is the worst thing that can happen to him. Rating something as bad involves using a rating scale of 0–99 per cent bad, while rating something as awful involves using a scale that is over 100 per cent bad. There is no logical connection between the two scales.

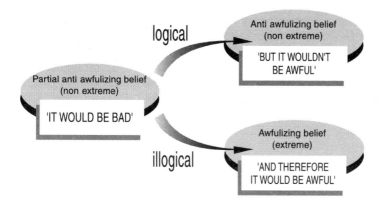

Applying the three arguments to low frustration tolerance beliefs (LFT)

If you recall from Chapter 2, when you hold an LFT belief you believe that you cannot tolerate the event about which you are depressed. Brian's LFT belief is expressed as: *I could not tolerate the loss of my useful role.*

- *Is this belief helpful?*
  Answer: No, because believing that he cannot tolerate the pending loss of his useful role leads to an unhealthy emotion of depression. Associated with Brian's depression are the behavioural consequences of withdrawing from his family, refusing to talk about his feelings and drinking more alcohol, all of which maintain depression and ultimately block Brian from focusing on developing other potentially useful roles.

- *Is this belief true?*
  Answer: No, because while it is true that Brian may have difficulty tolerating the loss of his useful role in the community he cannot prove that he cannot tolerate it. The belief *I cannot tolerate losing my useful role in the community* points to one of two things: either that he will die as a direct result of losing this role or that he will be prevented from ever experiencing happiness again.

So the LFT belief is inconsistent with reality, because even if Brian tells himself that he cannot stand losing this role he will not die as a direct result or forfeit future happiness.

- *Is this belief logical?*
  Answer: No, because while the realistic *non-extreme* evaluation that he may find the loss of a useful role difficult is logical, the *extreme* conclusion that he *cannot* tolerate it is illogical.

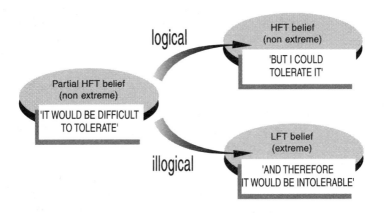

Using the three arguments with self-depreciation beliefs

Self-depreciation beliefs are global negative ratings of oneself. As you may recall, Brian's self-depreciation belief is: *Losing my useful role would prove that I am totally useless.*

- *Is this belief helpful?*
  Answer: No, as Brian feels depressed and with that predicts a negative future, and while he fears relying on his family, his emotions and behaviours make it more difficult for him to develop other interests outside his work and potentially find other roles in his community.

- *Is this belief true?*
  Answer: No, this belief is not true as Brian is a fallible, complex and unique human being made up of many characteristics. If Brian's belief that he is totally useless were true, then everything

about Brian would be useless; everything he has done, everything he now does and everything he will do would be totally useless. Since this is not true, even though he may feel useless he cannot truthfully describe himself as totally useless.

- *Is this belief logical?*
  Answer: No. Here, Brian demonstrates the part–whole error in his thinking. This involves identifying a part of yourself with which you are unhappy (in this case losing a useful role in the community) and generalizing this to your total self. Brian cannot legitimately rate himself totally on the basis of a change to one aspect (or even a few aspects) of his life.

Using the three major arguments with rational beliefs

The three arguments show how irrational beliefs are unhelpful, unscientific and illogical. These arguments can also be applied to the rational beliefs to test their rationality. This process can increase your understanding and your conviction. Earlier in this section we showed you the rational belief alternatives to Brian's depression-promoting irrational beliefs. In order for Brian to gain intellectual insight he needs to understand fully the rationality of the rational beliefs.

Using the three arguments with preferences

The rational alternative to demanding beliefs is preference beliefs; Brian's preferential belief is: *I don't want to lose my role in the community but there is no law that states this must not happen.*

- *Is this belief helpful?*
  Answer: Yes, because according to REBT theory, rational beliefs tend to produce healthy negative emotions such as sadness. With a healthy emotion of sadness Brian is more likely to have thinking consequences that are helpful, such as seeing both negative and positive aspects in the future. He is also more likely to have action tendencies that are helpful, such as seeking out other interests and reducing his alcohol intake.

- *Is this belief true?*

  Answer: Yes, because Brian can prove that he does not want to lose his useful role, and he can also prove that there is no law that prevents this from happening because, if there were such a law, he would be prevented from losing this role. Since he is not prevented, the preference belief is accurate.

- *Is this belief logical?*

  Answer: Yes, because it logically follows that what Brian wants doesn't have to happen. So, because he doesn't want to lose his useful role in the community, this does not mean that he *must* not. Both parts of the belief are flexible and are connected by their flexibility.

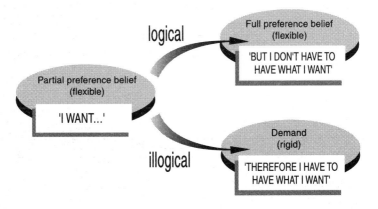

Using the three arguments with anti-awfulizing

The rational alternative to awfulizing is anti-awfulizing. As we discussed earlier, this involves rating the situation on a scale of 1–99.9 per cent bad. In Brian's case his anti-awfulizing belief is: *If I lose my useful role this would be bad, but if I put this into perspective, it is not the worst thing that could happen to me.*

- *Is this belief helpful?*

  Answer: Yes, because Brian's belief that his situation is bad but not the worst thing that can happen to him is conducive to the healthy negative emotion of sadness and the associated helpful

behaviours and thinking consequences. In short, the anti-awfulizing belief helps Brian to adjust to his pending retirement.

- *Is this belief consistent with reality?*
  Answer: Yes, because Brian can prove that losing his useful role is
  bad (on the scale of 1–99.9 per cent) as he is losing something that
  is important to him that he would prefer not to lose. Though he
  may feel as though his situation is extremely bad, he can prove
  that it is not the worst thing that could happen to him (i.e. 100 per
  cent bad).

- *Is this belief logical?*
  Answer: Yes, because the belief that his situation is bad is a non-
  extreme statement, and the conclusion that losing his role is not
  the worst thing that can happen is also non-extreme. As logical
  thinking is demonstrated through consistent statements, Brian's
  belief is logical because there is a non-extreme start and a non-
  extreme conclusion.

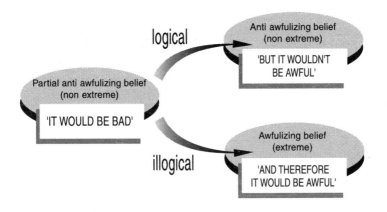

Using the three major arguments with high frustration tolerance (HFT)

As you may recall, Brian's rational belief is: *I may find it difficult to tolerate but I can tolerate it, and tolerating will help me to adjust to my retirement and focus on developing other interests.*

- *Is this belief helpful?*
  Answer: Yes, because when you hold HFT beliefs you tend to experience more productive results than unproductive ones. So Brian is more likely to adjust to his retirement, which is an unchangeable event. He is also more likely to focus on developing other interests once retired.

- *Is this belief true?*
  Answer: Yes. As Brian has spent much of his life working and his work has been of great importance to him, he is likely to find it difficult to tolerate losing this role. It is also true to say that he will tolerate it. Even if he does not tolerate the loss as he would like, he nevertheless tolerates it. It is also true to say that his reminding himself that he will tolerate this difficult situation will help him to focus on developing other interests.

- *Is this belief logical?*
  Answer: Yes, because the specific belief about pending retirement is healthy as it logically follows from the general HFT philosophy that he doesn't want to lose his useful role. There is a logical connection between saying something is difficult to tolerate and saying that it is tolerable, since both statements are non-extreme.

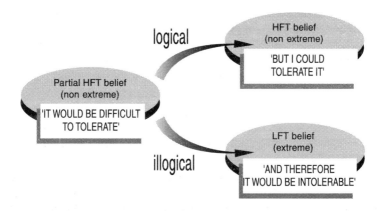

Using the three arguments with self-acceptance beliefs

The healthy negative emotion of sadness can occur when self-acceptance beliefs are employed. Brian's self-acceptance belief was: *If I were to lose my useful role in the community then this would not render me totally useless. There is more to me than my work and I cannot legitimately rate myself totally on whether I'm retired or not.*

- *Is this belief helpful?*
  Answer: Yes, because self-acceptance beliefs tend to produce the healthy negative emotion of sadness. This in turn yields constructive behavioural consequences and thinking consequences. As a result, Brian is more likely to achieve his goals to spend time with his family, reduce his alcohol intake and focus on developing other interests.

- *Is this belief true?*
  Answer: Yes, because although his useful role as a bank manager is an important aspect of Brian's life, it is not the only one. So he is correct in his belief that he cannot legitimately rate himself as totally useless in this one aspect.

- *Is this belief logical?*
  Answer: Yes, because the conclusion that he is a fallible human being is consistent with the belief that he will lose a useful role by retiring. He is also demonstrating good logic by stating that his work is one part of him and he cannot legitimately rate the whole of himself by a part of himself.

Summary

So far in this book Brian has gone through a number of steps to reach the point where he has what REBT refers to as intellectual insight. This means that Brian has an understanding of his activating event and the beliefs that largely determine his depression (as discussed in Chapter 2). In this chapter he has reviewed his ABC and challenged his rational and irrational beliefs. Using this chapter you can challenge your own beliefs following the same steps as Brian:

Step 1   Review your ABC.
Step 2   Consider the central role that irrational beliefs play in your depression.
Step 3   Consider the central role that rational beliefs play in healthy sadness.
Step 4   Recognize that the aim of challenging your beliefs is to understand the solution to your depression.
Step 5   Challenge your irrational beliefs with the three main arguments.
Step 6   Challenge your rational beliefs with the three main arguments.

A summary of all the stages involved in overcoming your depression will be presented later in this book.

Now that we have looked at the different arguments used to challenge the irrational and rational beliefs, you will hopefully have a better understanding of what makes irrational beliefs irrational and what makes rational beliefs rational. As you work through this book you may find it helpful to re-read sections, and when you challenge your own beliefs about specific situations you may find it helpful to refer to this chapter.

As we discussed earlier, assessing your ABC and challenging the irrational beliefs are unlikely to be enough for you to overcome your depression. In the next chapter we will show you how you can integrate rational beliefs into your own belief system and gain what is referred to as emotional insight.

5

How to Integrate Rational Beliefs into Your Belief System

Introduction

In Chapter 4 we showed you how you can gain an understanding of why irrational beliefs are irrational and why rational beliefs are rational. This is known as intellectual insight. At this point you may understand why your rational beliefs are rational, but it is likely that your understanding will be occasional, light and usually when you are not facing the activating event. Furthermore, your understanding may only have a minimal effect on your thoughts, feelings and behaviours. So when facing the same activating events you may still feel depressed and engage in self-defeating behaviours. In this chapter we aim to show you some techniques used in REBT to help you integrate rational beliefs into your belief system and gain emotional insight. So when faced with an activating event you will employ your rational beliefs and experience the healthy negative emotion of sadness and engage in helpful behaviours.

The difference between intellectual and emotional insight

Intellectual insight is important, but not enough to bring about the change from the unhealthy negative emotion of depression to the healthy negative emotion of sadness.

When people gain intellectual insight they say things like 'I know it in my mind but don't feel it in my gut.' This stage is normal, and equivalent situations occur in many aspects of life. Consider how you would go about improving your physical health. You may think a healthy diet and exercise would be helpful. Suppose you are thorough and refer to relevant literature or seek a professional consultation from a dietician. Would this knowledge of the best way to improve your physical health be enough to improve your health?

Of course not! You would need to act on the advice by changing your diet and taking part in an exercise programme. In order to get fit you would continue the healthy regime regularly for a sustained period. To stay fit for life you need to maintain the regime for life. It is the same with your mental health. In order to gain emotional insight you need to act on your intellectual insight and keep acting on your intellectual insight until you are mentally fit. In Chapter 9 we will show you some more techniques to help prevent relapse and help you stay mentally fit for life.

In this chapter we will introduce some exercises that can help you integrate your intellectual insight into your belief system, gain emotional insight and improve your mental fitness. In preparation for these exercises there are a number of important points to consider in order to increase your chances of being successful in overcoming your depression.

Develop your persuasive arguments

In Chapter 4 we looked at the three major arguments that question whether your belief about your activating event is helpful, truthful and logical. You may have noticed that you found some arguments easier to follow than others. For example, you may find pragmatic arguments easier than logical arguments. If this is the case then you can choose to use arguments that have the most impact on your beliefs. In addition to choosing the most persuasive arguments, you may help yourself by developing as many persuasive arguments as you can. Imagine you are on trial for a serious crime and you employ a lawyer to defend you. Would you rather she declines the opportunity to dismantle the prosecution's evidence and offers little evidence in your defence? Or would you rather she thoroughly dismantles the prosecution's evidence and offers as many persuasive arguments as she can to demonstrate your innocence? Which approach is more likely to persuade the jury of your innocence? Of course, the second approach is most likely to get you off the hook. It is the same with your beliefs. The more you dismantle your irrational beliefs and develop persuasive arguments in favour of rational beliefs, the more likely you are to integrate the rational solution into your belief system.

Act against your irrational beliefs in ways consistent with your developing rational beliefs

Remember Brian, whom we discussed in Chapter 4. He questioned his beliefs about losing a useful role in his community by asking whether the beliefs he held were helpful and truthful, and he concluded that his irrational beliefs were unhelpful, untruthful and illogical. However, his rational beliefs were helpful, truthful and logical. Let us suppose that after all the effort Brian has put into disputing his irrational beliefs and developing his rational beliefs, he continues to withdraw from his family, refuse to talk about his feelings and, in relation to his retirement, drink alcohol to drown his sorrows. How likely is it that he will integrate his rational beliefs into his belief system and overcome his depression? As you can imagine, it is unlikely that Brian will gain emotional insight. Now let's suppose that Brian acts in accordance with his developing rational beliefs and starts to talk to appropriate people about his feelings about his retirement, spends time with his family and stops using alcohol to drown his sorrows. These actions are much more likely to help him integrate his rational beliefs into his belief system and help him gain emotional insight and overcome his depression.

Do things uncomfortably and unconfidently and put up with feeling unnatural

During the process of integrating rational beliefs into your belief system you may experience a measure of discomfort; you may also lack confidence in the tasks designed to facilitate integration, and you may feel unnatural. These three phenomena are entirely normal at the integration stage, as you are forcing yourself to act and think differently without feeling any differently. Remember, your feelings will change quite a bit later. However, if you expect that you will feel unnatural, unconfident and uncomfortable and continue to work towards integration this phase will pass and you will eventually feel natural, gain confidence and feel comfortable in the steps designed to facilitate integration. Consider how you would feel if, after years of writing with your right hand, you learn to write with your left, or if you start to learn a new language, or adjust your golf swing after years of play. As a general rule we do things uncomfortably, unconfidently and unnaturally before we do them comfortably, confidently and naturally. If you remember this you will persist at the tasks designed to facilitate integration.

Understand and deal with obstacles

Because you are human and the process of helping yourself to overcome depression can in itself become a source of activating events and irrational beliefs, you may encounter obstacles to integration. In Chapter 7 we will show how you can overcome emotional problems about depression such as anxiety, guilt and shame. You can help yourself if you identify and deal with these obstacles. To help you in this endeavour here are two of the most common irrational beliefs that can be obstacles to completing integration exercises.

I must succeed in the task

This is a common irrational belief; you may be particularly prone to this irrational belief if you identified with the autonomy-type characteristics described in Chapter 1. This irrational belief is an obstacle because, as with all irrational beliefs, it underpins unhealthy negative emotions such as depression and anxiety, thus creating more emotional disturbance. It is also inconsistent with reality as there is no universal law that dictates that you must succeed at the task. If there were, then it would be impossible to fail. Since that is not true the belief is irrational. In addition to this, the belief yields unhealthy results because, while you are concentrating on whether you are succeeding at the task, you are not concentrating on the task itself.

I must be motivated to do something before I do it

This irrational belief can be an obstacle to carrying out integration activities for a number of reasons. First, because if you are depressed you are likely to feel unmotivated and if you wait to feel motivated then you will wait a long time. If you recall from Chapter 1, action comes before motivation, so in order to get motivated you need to take action. Second, this belief is not helpful as it yields poor results in that it can hinder you from taking the necessary steps involved with integrating the rational solution and overcoming your depression.

Techniques for integration

There are many techniques you can use to help you integrate rational beliefs into your belief system. Below, we have described some of the most common and effective methods in REBT.

Attack–response technique

When you use this method it is best to use the form provided for this purpose (see Figure 5.1).

1 Start by writing your healthy sadness-creating belief in the space at the top of the left-hand column. Write down only one belief.
2 Rate your level of conviction in this belief on a scale of 1–100 per cent conviction in the space provided.
3 Attack your healthy belief, using arguments that form the core of the irrational beliefs that underpin your depression. Write one in the space in the right-hand column.
4 Defend your healthy belief against this attack. Make sure you answer every argument you used in the attack. Write down your defence in the next space down from the top left-hand column.
5 Then again attack this defence with more arguments based on the irrational beliefs that underpin your depression and write these down in the next space in the right-hand column.
6 Continue in this vein until you have answered all your attacks. You may need many forms for this purpose. Finally, re-rate your conviction in the original healthy belief that you wrote at the top of the left-hand page.

If you have followed the above stages properly you should have increased your level of conviction to that of healthy belief. Figure 5.2 shows Brian's attack–response form.

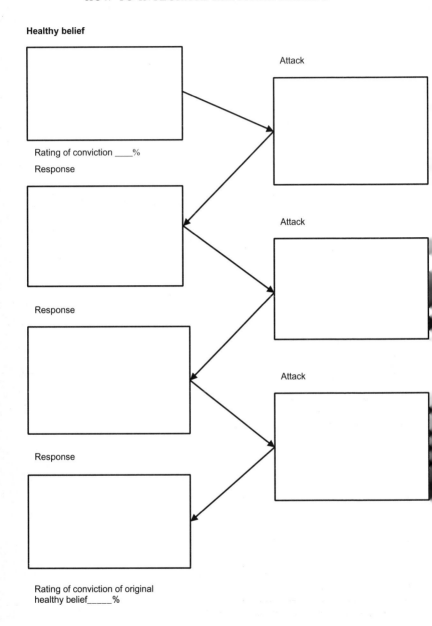

Figure 5.1   Blank attack–response form

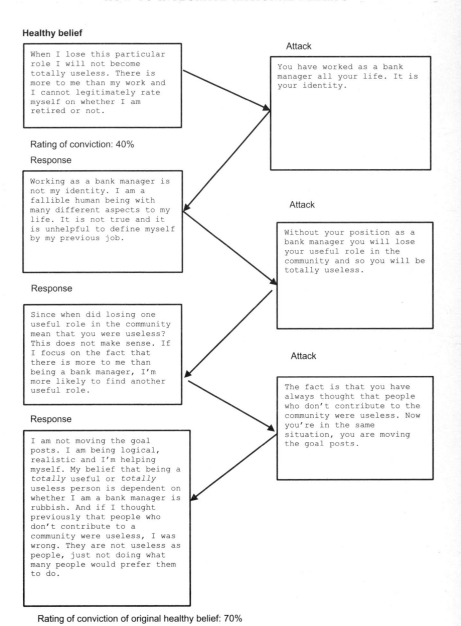

Healthy belief

When I lose this particular role I will not become totally useless. There is more to me than my work and I cannot legitimately rate myself on whether I am retired or not.

Rating of conviction: 40%

Response

Working as a bank manager is not my identity. I am a fallible human being with many different aspects to my life. It is not true and it is unhelpful to define myself by my previous job.

Response

Since when did losing one useful role in the community mean that you were useless? This does not make sense. If I focus on the fact that there is more to me than being a bank manager, I'm more likely to find another useful role.

Response

I am not moving the goal posts. I am being logical, realistic and I'm helping myself. My belief that being a *totally* useful or *totally* useless person is dependent on whether I am a bank manager is rubbish. And if I thought previously that people who don't contribute to a community were useless, I was wrong. They are not useless as people, just not doing what many people would prefer them to do.

Attack

You have worked as a bank manager all your life. It is your identity.

Attack

Without your position as a bank manager you will lose your useful role in the community and so you will be totally useless.

Attack

The fact is that you have always thought that people who don't contribute to the community were useless. Now you're in the same situation, you are moving the goal posts.

Rating of conviction of original healthy belief: 70%

Figure 5.2   Brian's attack–response form

Rational-emotive imagery (REI)

Rational-emotive imagery draws on the capacity that humans have to use their imagination for better or worse. Thus we may imagine a negative activating event happening (A) and bring our irrational belief (B) to this imagined event, thus creating emotional disturbance at C. However, if we use our capacity for imagery for the worse we can also use it for the better. So while imagining the same activating event, we can practise thinking rationally about it and create a healthy emotional and behavioural response.

There are two versions of rational-emotive imagery:

Version 1

In this version of REI, close your eyes and imagine you are confronting the activating event (point A in the ABC) about which you made yourself depressed. Imagine this event as vividly as you can, and make yourself feel depressed. Then, while still imagining the activating event as clearly as you can, change your feelings from unhealthy depression to healthy sadness. When you have done this, notice what you did to bring about this emotional change. You probably did this by changing your irrational depression-creating beliefs to rational sadness-creating beliefs. If this method is helpful to you and you are at the stage where you want to integrate your rational beliefs into your belief system, then practise this exercise 20 minutes per day.

Version 2

In this version of REI, close your eyes and imagine that you are confronting the activating event (point A in the ABC model) about which you made yourself depressed. Imagine this event as vividly as you can and make yourself feel depressed. Do this by rehearsing your irrational belief. Then, while still imagining this event as clearly as you can, change your feelings from unhealthy depression to healthy sadness by rehearsing the healthy beliefs that underpin your sadness. Practise this version for 20 minutes per day.

These versions of REI give you the opportunity to change your unhealthy depression to healthy sadness by changing the unhealthy beliefs to healthy beliefs. The methods help you deepen your conviction in the beliefs that underpin healthy sadness. Here is how Brian used REI, explained in his own words:

> *I closed my eyes and I pictured myself after my retirement. I imagined myself sat at home in the lounge on my own. While seeing this in my mind's eye, I told myself that I must not lose my useful role in the community and that I am totally useless. I made myself feel depressed. Then, while still imagining myself sat at home, I told myself that I didn't want to lose my useful role in the community but that there is no law that states this must not happen. I also told myself that I am not useless and cannot legitimately rate myself on whether I am retired or working at the bank. I noticed that while practising the rational beliefs my depression changed to healthy sadness.*

Notice that Brian used version 2. He practised his REI exercise for 10 minutes in the morning and 10 minutes in the evening.

Rational self-statements

In our experience, some clients have found it useful to write down rational beliefs on small cards, particularly when starting to integrate their rational beliefs into their belief system. You can keep these in your pocket or bag and consult them when you have difficulty recalling the rational beliefs.

Summary

The integration techniques described in this chapter are designed to help you integrate the rational beliefs into your own belief system and develop emotional insight. We have described the attack–response method, rational-emotive imagery and rational self-statements. It is likely that you will need to repeat the exercises and act in accordance with rational beliefs for some time to gain emotional insight. In addition to this we highlighted the importance of:

1 developing your persuasive arguments for rational beliefs and against irrational beliefs;

2 persisting with the integration tasks even if at first you lack confidence in the task, or feel uncomfortable or unnatural;

3 understanding and dealing with obstacles to integration such as any irrational beliefs you may have about completing integration tasks.

In the next chapter we will show you how you can deal with the thinking consequences of depression.

6

Overcoming the Thinking Consequences of Depression

Introduction

In the previous chapter we showed you how you can integrate rational beliefs into your belief system, using a number of different strategies to question your irrational beliefs and act in accordance with your rational beliefs. Once you have successfully worked through these important stages with a specific problem situation pertaining to your depression, you are ready to question the thinking consequences of your depression. In this chapter we will highlight the thinking consequences of depression and then suggest some strategies that can help you overcome this depression-derived thinking. Finally, we will reconsider inferences made at point A (activating event) in the ABC of depression. We will refer to Maxine, whom we met in Chapter 1, to illustrate these points.

Depression, as we have discussed it in this book, is the consequence (C) of an activating event (A) about which you have irrational beliefs (B) i.e. A→B→C. When you experience depression you tend to think in distorted ways, as we discussed in Chapter 3. The thinking consequences in themselves can become activating events, and when these events are evaluated by irrational rigid beliefs such as demands, they can result in more depression. The problem does not end here, as again depression-related thinking consequences can serve as additional activating events to be evaluated with irrational beliefs, and thus more depression and more distorted thinking, and so the vicious cycle of depression can continue. Bearing this in mind, rather than the ABC process being linear, as described above, it is more realistic to show the process as a cycle, as shown in Figure 6.1.

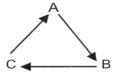

Figure 6.1 ABC process as a cycle

The following are typical examples of depression-influenced thinking consequences or inferences. To illustrate how thinking consequences can maintain and intensify depression we will use Maxine's case.

Depression-derived inferences

Only seeing negative aspects of the loss or failure

Maxine had demanded that she must not fail, and in her eyes anything less than three A grades would be failure. When Maxine received her results she did not notice the two A grade results but focused on the one B grade. This grade was lower than she had expected, although to many this would still be a respectable pass. The significance is that her demand that she must do perfectly well had not been met; as such she felt depressed. While depressed she focused on the negative aspects of not attaining perfect grades. She inferred that her family and teachers were trying to reassure her but were actually hiding the fact that they also saw her results as failure. She inferred that because of her failure to achieve perfect results, her friends would think that her previous achievements had been due to chance rather than talent.

Thinking of other losses or failures one has experienced

While she was depressed Maxine spent long periods of time thinking back to other occasions when she had not achieved her goals. Although few and far between, these incidents were used by Maxine to support her self-depreciating belief that she was a failure. She focused on the two previous occasions when she had received B grades on assignments she had written. She remembered that she had to work harder than her friend James in physics class, but he had still gained a higher percentage than she had. The more Maxine thought about her past, the more failure incidents she could identify. These memories were inferences that served as activating events, and as she held on to the demanding belief, I must not fail, she felt increasingly depressed.

Thinking you are unable to help yourself (helplessness)

Maxine had revised for her exams and did not achieve her desired results of three A-grade A levels. She demanded that she *must not fail* and had planned a careful study regime and had maintained it. Despite these efforts she had not got the results she wanted, so in her view she had failed. While depressed about this she thought at length about how, despite her efforts, she had not succeeded. If she had not succeeded before, then in her view she was not able to help herself and influence the outcome, and she thus inferred she would be helpless in preventing herself failing in the future. As she inferred she *must not fail*, there was no point in studying and she gave in to her inference that she was helpless and refused to continue.

Anticipating that the future will be painful and bleak (hopelessness)

Despite reassurance from her family, Maxine predicted that she would be destined to fail in the future. She thought that any further attempt to pass her A levels – in fact, any academic study – would be met by failure. She inferred: *I have failed so I will always fail. I will never be able to fulfil my dream of going to Cambridge to study medicine and become a doctor.* Maxine inferred that her future was hopeless; the more she ruminated, the worse her future looked, and as these thoughts became activating events for her belief that she *must not fail*, her depression intensified.

Maxine's experience illustrates how when you feel depressed you are vulnerable to further depression and getting caught in the vicious cycle of depression. In order to break this cycle of disturbance it is important to assess your activating event and assume temporarily that it is true. This then helps you identify the associated irrational beliefs when you experience depressed mood. Once you have completed this, follow the stages of questioning irrational beliefs, establishing rational belief alternatives and using techniques to integrate the rational alternatives detailed in Chapters 4 and 5. Only when you have completed this process do you return to your depression-related inferences and question their accuracy.

Thinking consequences of healthy sadness

If you are successful in completing the stages described in Chapters 4 and 5 (challenging your specific irrational beliefs, developing rational beliefs and integrating them into your belief system) you are likely to feel sad rather than depressed when faced with the same or similar activating events. When Maxine worked through the stages detailed in Chapters 4 and 5 and established a healthy emotional consequence of sadness, her thinking consequences were functional. This meant she was able to return to her studies. To demonstrate this, consider the following thinking consequences of sadness illustrated by Maxine's case:

1 *You are able to see both positive and negative aspects of the loss or failure*
 Maxine was able to see that, on the one hand, it was negative that she had not attained the marks she wanted. On the other hand, the positive aspects were that (a) she could learn from this failure, and (b) she had time to revise more subjects before the finals.
2 *You are less likely to think of other losses or failures than when depressed*
 Maxine found that when she felt sad about the failure to get the grades she wanted she did not spend her time ruminating about other occasions when she had not done as well as she wanted.
3 *You think you are able to help yourself*
 Maxine used the experience to her advantage and considered new strategies for her revision, such as adding some additional subject areas to her revision as an insurance policy. She also decided to book a tutorial with her teacher to advise her on how she could improve her study skills.

66

4 *You are able to look to the future with hope*
Maxine renewed her interest in going to Cambridge to study medicine; she also considered other universities in case she did not get the grades she hoped for.

Questioning your thinking consequences

Once you have successfully challenged irrational beliefs and acted on your rational beliefs you are in a position to stand back and consider the truth of the depression-derived inferences. Feeling sad but not depressed will help you to be objective about your depression-derived inferences.

When challenging your depression-related inferences, here are some useful questions to ask yourself:

1 How realistic is my thinking?
2 How else can I view this?
3 How likely is it to be true?
4 If I asked someone whom I trust to give me an objective opinion about my inference, what would this person say to me?
5 If someone in the same situation told me they had this inference, what would I say to them about the validity of their inference?
6 Would twelve objective judges agree with my inference?
7 What inference would these twelve objective judges make instead?
8 What data do I need to gather to check the validity of my inference and how reliable would this data be?

Once Maxine had gone through the process of assessing her specific ABC and challenged her irrational beliefs, formed rational beliefs and acted on them, she revisited her depression-derived inferences and questioned the validity of the thinking consequences.

Inference 1 **My family and teachers think I'm a failure**
Question: How realistic is my thinking here?
Response: No one has said they think I'm a failure or that I failed. On the

67

contrary, the evidence I have is that they are pleased with my result (even if I'm not) and don't understand my disappointment. Going by the observed evidence my inference is unrealistic.

Inference 2 **My friends think my previous results were due to chance, not talent**

Question: How else can I view this?

Response: There are alternative ways of viewing this: one is that they think that my previous achievements have been because of ability; another could be that they view my previous achievements as a result of hard work. Alternatively, they may have thought my previous achievements to be a combination of the first two reasons, so I cannot legitimately support my inference as the only way to view this.

Inference 3 **There is no point in trying because I can't do anything to influence the outcome**

Question: If someone in the same situation as me told me they had this inference, what would I say to them about the validity of the inference?

Response: If someone said that to me, they would have difficulty persuading me that their inference was valid. Sure, they may think they can't do anything to influence the outcome but does that really mean they can't influence it? Of course not! There may not be a guarantee of success but there are still things you can do to improve your chances of success.

Inference 4 **I have failed so I will always fail**

Question: What data do I need to gather to check the validity of this inference and how reliable would this data be?

Response: In order to prove this inference the data would be all my previous actions. All of these would need to be actions that have failed. As this is not the case, my inference is not valid. The other data would be all my future actions, and as I do not know what will happen with any certainty I don't have access to this data, so I cannot reliably check the validity of the inference.

Reconsider inferences that are held at A

As we discussed in Chapter 2, activating events can be inferences, and at this point we asked you to assume that the inference is true. The reason for this is that inferences are not enough to bring about depression; this is done when you evaluate the inference with irrational beliefs (see Chapter 2). For example, Maxine has an inference at point A: *I have failed*. She evaluates this inference with irrational beliefs such as *I must not fail* and *This proves I'm a failure*. So she is likely to experience depression as a consequence, with associated behaviours and further inferences.

Following the assessment and challenging process detailed in Chapter 4 Maxine has the same inference: *I have failed*. She evaluates the inference with rational beliefs such as *I don't want to fail but am not immune from failing* and *If I fail this does not prove I'm a failure but rather a fallible human being capable of both success and failure*. This means she is more likely to experience healthy sadness and is less likely to have distorted thinking consequences.

If you were to question the inference that serves as the activating event before challenging your irrational beliefs, you may feel less depressed but would not have reached the core of the depression, the irrational beliefs. Assuming that the inference is true helps you to identify the irrational beliefs at the heart of your depression and means you are less vulnerable to future depression when in the same situation. If you were to bypass the irrational beliefs in the process of overcoming depression, your views about yourself, others and the world would still be influenced by the ongoing existence of the irrational belief.

Once you have worked through your irrational beliefs successfully you are in a better position to question the inference that served as the activating event. To question the inference you can use the questions we detailed on p. 66. In Maxine's case, she questioned her initial inference that she had failed because she did not achieve the grades she wanted.

Inference   **I have failed**
Question: How else can I view this?
Response: Another way of viewing this is to say that I have not done as
                well as I wanted, and as this was an important exam for me
                I'm sad about it. But not doing as well as I wanted does not
                mean that I failed: I still passed and there may be something I
                can learn from this experience that will help me in the future.

Summary

In this chapter we have shown you how the thinking consequences of depression can become activating events and maintain a vicious cycle of depression. We also described some of the common thinking consequences of depression and some strategies for questioning the inferences that are consequences of depression and activating events for depression.

So far in this book we have addressed the REBT assessment and treatment of depression. For some people, accessing their activating events and beliefs that result in depression can be made more difficult because their most pressing problem is the way they think and feel about being depressed. In the next chapter we will address emotional problems about depression that occur when people hold irrational beliefs about their experience of depression.

7

Overcoming Emotional Problems about Depression

Introduction

Depression rarely exists as an unhealthy emotion in isolation; it is more common that depression will exist along with other unhealthy negative emotions such as anxiety, guilt and shame. In many cases people disturb themselves about being depressed. In the last chapter we showed you how your thinking consequences of depression can serve as activating events for further depression and thus maintain or even increase the intensity of your depression. In this chapter we will show you, first, how you can use the ABC framework to assess your emotional problems when you experience other unhealthy negative emotions about depression. Second, we will show you how you can overcome associated emotional problems by using the steps already covered in this book. Finally, we will show you when you need to take the necessary steps to overcome your emotional problems about depression before you tackle your depression. As before, we will use cases to illustrate our points. In this chapter we will see how Sylvia, Maxine, Brian, Neelam and Colin overcame their emotional problems about depression.

REBT theory states that when people have emotional or behavioural problems such as depression, they often disturb themselves about these problems. We call these meta-emotional problems because they are literally emotional problems about emotional problems. So this means that the emotional consequence of your depression is likely to serve as an activating event, and if you hold irrational and unhealthy beliefs about this activating event of depression you are likely to experience additional emotional problems. Below are some of the most common emotional reactions to depression that we have encountered in therapeutic practice.

Anxiety about depression

REBT theory describes anxiety as an unhealthy negative emotion that occurs when you hold irrational beliefs about an activating event concerned with threat or danger. So, with a second-order problem of anxiety, you view the emotion of depression as the threatening or dangerous activating event. As we have already discussed in this book, depression is the unhealthy negative emotion and the healthy negative emotion alternative is sadness. Where the problem emotion is anxiety, the healthy negative emotion is concern. You can distinguish between healthy and unhealthy negative emotions by checking for the presence of either functional or dysfunctional thinking and behavioural consequences, as below.

Thinking consequences of anxiety

- Overestimating the negative features of the threat.
- Underestimating the ability to cope with the threat.
- Creating an even more negative threat in one's mind.
- Having more difficulty concentrating on tasks and being more likely to be distracted by thoughts of the threat than when concerned.

Thinking consequences of concern

- Viewing the threat realistically.
- Realistically appraising one's ability to cope with the threat.
- Not creating an even more negative threat in one's mind.
- Having increased ability to concentrate and being less distracted by the threat than when anxious.

Behavioural consequences (action tendencies) of anxiety

- Withdrawing physically from the threat.
- Withdrawing mentally from the threat.
- Warding off the threat (e.g. by superstitious behaviour).
- Tranquillizing feelings.
- Seeking reassurance.

Behavioural consequences (action tendencies) of concern

- Facing up to the threat.
- Dealing with the threat constructively.

Behavioural consequences of emotions may not be acted on, and sometimes these behaviours are what you want to do rather than what you actually do. As such they are sometimes called action tendencies. It is also worth noting that not everyone who experiences anxiety or concern uses these words to describe their emotions. For example, some people say 'fear' instead of 'anxiety'.

We met Sylvia in Chapter 1. Her depression was triggered when she inferred that her family no longer needed her and that she had lost her helping role. As she held irrational beliefs that she had to be helpful, and that if she was not helpful then she had no worth, she soon felt depressed. When Sylvia thought about her depression she viewed it as a potential threat to her future happiness and told herself that she must never be depressed again. The demanding belief that she must not be depressed resulted in anxiety about the possibility that she might be depressed in the future. While anxious she predicted that she would be unable to cope with depression and imagined that her depression would be more intense in the future, even to the point where she would attempt suicide.

Sylvia had lacked energy and had more difficulty eating, drinking and washing while depressed. So, when anxious about depression, she tended to interpret innocuous changes in appetite and energy levels as a sign that her depression was returning. She asked her husband to reassure her that he had not noticed her symptoms returning. His reassurance helped to reduce her anxious feelings in the short term. However, Sylvia realized it was not enough to guarantee that she would never be depressed in the future so she was soon anxious again.

From this description we can be sure that Sylvia is anxious rather than concerned about being depressed in the future, because she has some (but not all) of the thinking and behavioural consequences associated with anxiety. Using the ABC framework for assessing emotional problems, her meta-emotional problem of anxiety is illustrated below:

A1 = I have lost my helping role.
B1 = I must not lose my helping role. As I have I am worthless.
C1 = Depression.
↓

A2 = If I am depressed in the future I may try to commit suicide.

B2 = I must know for sure that I will not be depressed or suicidal in the future.

C2 = Anxious (seeks reassurance from her husband).

Sylvia's goal will be to be sad rather than depressed about the possibility of feeling depressed in the future. We will show you how to overcome the second-order problem later in this chapter.

Unhealthy anger about depression

If you identified with the description of autonomous characteristics in Chapter 2 then you are likely to demand that you should not be depressed and possibly put yourself down as weak or incompetent for experiencing depression. In such cases you may feel unhealthy anger towards yourself. REBT distinguishes between healthy and unhealthy anger in terms of the thinking and behavioural consequences.

Healthy and unhealthy anger are responses to activating events concerning (1) frustration; (2) transgressing a personal rule; or (3) threats to self-esteem. The deciding factor in whether the emotional consequence is healthy or unhealthy is whether the beliefs about the activating event are rational or irrational.

Thinking consequences of unhealthy anger

- Overestimating the extent to which an act is deliberate.
- Seeing malicious intent in the motives behind the act.
- Seeing yourself as definitely right and others as definitely wrong.
- Not being able to see others' point of view.
- Plotting to exact revenge.

Thinking consequences of healthy anger

- Not overestimating the extent to which the act was deliberate.
- Not seeing malicious intent in the motives of others.
- Not seeing yourself as definitely right and others as definitely wrong.
- Able to see another person's point of view.

- Not plotting to exact revenge.

Behavioural consequences (action tendencies) of unhealthy anger

- Attacking yourself or the other person physically.
- Attacking yourself or the other person verbally.
- Attacking the other person passive aggressively.
- Displacing the attack on to another person, animal or object.
- Withdrawing aggressively.
- Recruiting allies against others.

Behavioural consequences (action tendencies) of healthy anger

- Asserting yourself with others.
- Requesting, but not demanding, a behaviour change from others.

As you can see from the description of the thoughts and behaviours that are the consequences of healthy and unhealthy anger, many of them relate to the actions of others. Sometimes you may direct the second-order problem of depression at yourself, and this is termed *unhealthy ego anger*. In these cases you consider that you have violated one of your own rules or standards. Such violations may refer to acts of commission (when you break your own rule by doing something) or acts of omission (when you break your own rule by failing to do something).

In Maxine's case, she experienced unhealthy anger when she demanded that she should not have allowed herself to be depressed, as this was proof that she was weak. As you will remember, Maxine has high and exacting standards for her performance academically; she also has high and exacting standards for her behaviour. When she failed to attain the grades she wanted (and demanded of herself), she interpreted this as failing, and she then activated the irrational belief *I must not fail* which in turn resulted in depression. The depression then served as an activating event for her demanding belief that she absolutely shouldn't let herself be depressed as this was a sign of her weakness, and she then directed unhealthy anger towards herself by calling herself weak and pathetic, and on occasion she hit her fist against the wall. These thoughts and behaviours only add to the problems she faces and so are unhelpful in overcoming both her anger and her depression.

75

Using the ABC framework the second-order problem of unhealthy anger can be demonstrated as:

A1 = I have failed.
B1 = I must not fail; if I fail then that means I'm a failure.
C1 = Depression.
  ↓
A2 = Depression is a weakness.
B2 = I absolutely shouldn't allow myself to be weak.
C2 = Anger.

If you believe that you have a problem of anger and want to do something about it you may wish to consult *Overcoming Anger: When Anger Helps and When It Hurts* by Dr Windy Dryden (Sheldon Press, 1996).

Guilt about depression

Unhealthy ego anger can resemble guilt in that both emotions demand that you must act (or not act) in a certain way. The main difference is that in guilt you have broken a rule that relates to your moral code, whereas in unhealthy ego anger the broken rule tends not to relate to your moral code.

Guilt and the healthy negative emotion of remorse tend to be activated by events where you violate a moral code, fail to live up to a moral code or hurt the feelings of significant others. Whether the negative emotion is healthy or unhealthy depends on whether you evaluate the activating event with rational or irrational beliefs. You can identify whether you feel healthy remorse or unhealthy guilt by the thinking consequences and behaviour consequences described below.

Thinking consequences of guilt
- Assuming you have definitely committed the act of violation of, or failed to live up to, the moral code.
- Assuming more personal responsibility than the situation warrants.

- Assigning far less responsibility to others than is warranted.
- Not thinking of mitigating factors.
- Thinking that you will receive retribution.

Thinking consequences of remorse

- Considering your behaviour in context in making the final judgement as to whether you violated or failed to live up to your moral code.
- Assuming the appropriate level of personal responsibility.
- Assigning the appropriate level of responsibility to others.
- Taking into account mitigating factors.
- Not thinking you will receive retribution.

Behavioural consequences (action tendencies) of guilt

- Escaping from the unhealthy pain of guilt in self-defeating ways.
- Begging forgiveness from the person wronged.
- Promising unrealistically that you will not 'sin' again.
- Punishing yourself physically or by deprivation.
- Disclaiming responsibility for the wrongdoing.

Behavioural consequences (action tendencies) of remorse

- Facing up to the healthy pain that accompanies the realization that you have 'sinned'.
- Asking but not begging for forgiveness.
- Understanding the reasons for the wrongdoing and acting on your understanding.
- Atoning by taking a penalty.
- Making appropriate amends.
- Not making excuses for your behaviour and enacting other defensive behaviours.

Neelam was originally motivated by her interest in the welfare of others, but when she worked in the soup kitchen and compared the misfortunes of others to her own comparative comfort, she thought more and more about how unfair the world was. Her activating event was the apparent misfortune of others when they did not deserve such misfortune. As she held irrational beliefs that people absolutely shouldn't experience misfortune when they don't deserve it, she slumped into a depression and eventually stopped her charity work. Once depressed, Neelam began to disturb herself about the fact that she was depressed and told herself that she absolutely should not be depressed as there were others worse off than her. She concluded that, as she was depressed when others were worse off in the world, then she was a selfish and self-indulgent person. In response to these irrational beliefs Neelam felt guilty and started to use alcohol as a way of escaping from the pain of her guilt.

Using the ABC framework, the primary and secondary problem is illustrated as:

A1 = People experience misfortune who do not deserve to.
B1 = People absolutely should not experience misfortune when they don't deserve it.
C1 = Depression.
↓
A2 = Depression when others are worse off.
B2 = I absolutely should not be depressed, because there are others worse off than me. As I am depressed this makes me a selfish and self-indulgent person.
C2 = Guilt.

Shame about depression

You experience shame and disappointment when an event occurs where something 'shameful' has been revealed about you, either by yourself or by others, and you believe others will look down on you or shun you. In the case of depression, in many societies the fact that you are or have been depressed can have a stigma. So feelings of depression can be the event triggering the beliefs that result in shame or disappointment. As with all the healthy and unhealthy negative emotions we have discussed, the healthy negative emotion (in this case disappointment) is a result of holding rational beliefs about the activating event. The unhealthy negative emotion of shame is the result of holding irrational beliefs about the activating event. You can assess whether you are feeling shame or disappointment by checking whether you experience the thinking and behavioural consequences detailed below:

Thinking consequences of shame

- Overestimating the 'shamefulness' of the information revealed.
- Overestimating the likelihood that the judging group will notice or be interested in the information.
- Overestimating the degree of disapproval you will receive.
- Overestimating the length of time any disapproval will last.

Thinking consequences of disappointment

- Seeing the information revealed in a compassionate self-accepting context.
- Being realistic about the likelihood that the judging group will notice or be interested in the information.
- Being realistic about the degree of disapproval you will receive.
- Being realistic about the length of time any disapproval will last.

Behavioural consequences (action tendencies) of shame

- Removing yourself from the 'gaze' of others.
- Isolating yourself from others.
- Saving face by attacking others who revealed the 'shameful' information.
- Ignoring attempts by others to restore the social equilibrium.

Behavioural consequences (action tendencies) of disappointment

- Continuing to participate in social interaction.
- Responding to the attempts by others to restore the social equilibrium.

Brian experienced shame on being diagnosed by his GP as having depression. This shame was a second-order problem since it was as a result of the depression. Brian's initial emotional problem was depression; he was coming up to mandatory retirement and inferred that he would lose his useful role in the community. He held an irrational belief that he *must not lose his useful role in the community.* When he experienced depression and, importantly, when his GP diagnosed him as depressed he told himself that he must not be depressed and that if he were depressed that meant that he was a 'weak' man. He felt shame and did not tell anyone of the outcome of his consultation with his doctor, namely a prescription of anti-depressants. He also imagined that his local community would shun him, so he isolated himself. We know from this information that Brian experienced shame rather than regret about his depression as he has a number of thinking and behavioural consequences associated with shame. His primary and secondary problems can be represented using the ABC framework below:

A1 = I will lose my useful role in the community.
B1 = I must not lose my useful role in the community. It is the worst thing that could happen to me. I could not tolerate the loss – it would prove that I am totally useless.
C1 = Depression.
↓
A2 = Others will look down on me if they know I'm depressed.
B2 = Others must not look down on me; if they did it would be terrible.
C2 = Shame (keeps the diagnosis from the GP secret and hides his prescription, avoids social situations).

Depression about depression

Depression about being depressed or the possibility that you may at some time in the future experience depression is common, particularly for those people who have been depressed more than once. If you are depressed and you disturb yourself about this depression then this can double the dose of your depression. Overcoming depression about depression can be an important relapse prevention strategy. We will discuss relapse prevention in more detail in the next chapter.

At this stage in the book it is unlikely that you will need reminding of the thinking and behavioural consequences of depression and sadness, nor that irrational beliefs largely determine depression and rational beliefs largely determine sadness. However, if you need a refresher then refer to Chapter 2.

Colin was depressed about his depression. He had been depressed before, and during this episode of depression he demanded of himself that he must not be depressed and that this was weakness so he must therefore be weak. This depression in turn activated his belief that he must not be depressed in the future and that he could not bear being depressed. This resulted in even more depression. At this point of the vicious cycle of depression Colin is hopeless about the future and believes he is unable to help himself to overcome the depression. Thinking consequences of hopelessness have been thought to be associated with suicide attempts, so clearly addressing Colin's meta-emotional problem of depression is crucial to his eventual recovery.

His 'double' depression can be illustrated using the ABC framework below:

A1 = I am going to get depressed again.
B1 = I must not be depressed.
C1 = Depression.
    ↓
A2 = There is nothing I can do to stop feeling depressed.
B2 = I must be able to stop my feelings of depression. Not stopping my feeling of depression means that I am a weak man who has lost his ability to help himself and thus I will always be depressed.
C2 = Depression.

Overcoming emotional problems about depression

Once you have established that you have a second-order problem about depression, the next question is: which problem do you address first? As a general guide it is best to stick to dealing with the primary problem of depression first and then address the secondary problem, but there are some exceptions to this where you would be advised to deal with the second-order problem first:

1 *When the meta-emotional problem interferes with the work you are doing to address your problem of depression* For example, Brian's second-order problem of shame was accompanied by behavioural consequences of isolating himself and avoiding the 'gaze' of others. He also overestimated the extent to which others would judge him negatively. Brian's behavioural and thinking consequences of shame interfere with his ability to overcome his depression, as ideally he would aim to have more social contact

and seek out appropriate support. His shame-related inferences and behaviours make this more difficult; as such, it is in Brian's interest to tackle his shame first.

2 *When the meta-emotional problem is more severe than the primary problem of depression* If you recall from Chapter 1, depression can be mild, moderate or severe, but it is still an unhealthy negative emotion. Just as you can experience a mild or intense healthy sadness, the key to whether an emotion is healthy or unhealthy is whether the underlying beliefs are rational or irrational. So it is feasible that you can experience moderate depression with a severe meta-emotional problem of anxiety. In such cases it is appropriate to work through the second-order problem first. For example, if Sylvia's anxiety about developing a more severe depression in the future were more intense than the current episode of depression, it would be sensible to deal with the anxiety problem first.

Using REBT to overcome a second-order problem is the same as using REBT to overcome your primary depression.

Assess your emotional problem using the ABC framework described in Chapter 2

If you suspect the problem is something other than depression, you will need to refer to the different unhealthy (and healthy) emotions and subsequent thinking and behavioural consequences discussed in the earlier part of this chapter.

For example, Brian assessed his meta-emotional problem of shame by identifying shame-related thinking consequences and behaviours; his shame-related ABC framework is:

A2 = Others will look down on me if they know I'm depressed.
B2 = Others must not look down on me; if they did it would be terrible.
C2 = Shame (keeps the diagnosis from the GP secret and hides his prescription; avoids social situations).

Challenge your irrational and rational beliefs

Brian challenged his beliefs using scientific arguments and concluded:

Although it would be nice to have a guarantee preventing others from looking down on me I do not have one. While it may be a negative experience if others were to look down on me, I cannot conclude that it would be terrible as there are worse things that can happen. Besides, by telling myself that it would be terrible, I create more emotional problems for myself.

Act in accordance with your rational beliefs and use the other techniques described in Chapter 5

In Brian's case he told his wife about his meeting with the GP and showed her the prescription he had been given. She did not look down on him but encouraged him to take care of himself by taking the medication and offered her support should he need it.

Revisit inferences at point A and C in the ABC and question the validity of the inferences using the questions detailed in Chapter 6

Brian checked his inference that others would look down on him if they knew of his depression by asking himself some of the questions detailed in Chapter 6:

Question: How likely is this to be true?

Response: As my wife did not look down on me and she is the first (and most important) person I have told, then I cannot say my inference is true in all cases, though it may be true for some.

Question: How else can I view this?

Response: That some people may look down on me and some people won't. What is important is how I react to this problem, and avoiding social situations and not taking medication that may help me is not going to assist me to overcome my depression.

Assess for additional second-order problems and repeat the above process

Brian assessed for other meta-emotional problems and completed the above process for a meta-emotional problem of anger. As a result Brian is in a stronger position to overcome the primary problem of depression.

Summary

Having now considered second-order problems, what determines them, what the consequences are and how to deal with them, we are ready to look at some techniques for preventing future relapses and dealing with them if they occur.

8

Preventing Future Episodes of Depression

Introduction

There are some strategies that are specifically designed to help prevent future episodes of depression. In this chapter we will show you some preventative strategies commonly used in REBT. We will discuss how recurrent inferences and core beliefs can play a part in your vulnerability to depression and show you how to identify them, challenge them and change them.

Step 1: Identify situations that you feel depressed about

The first thing to do is to consider those situations that you feel depressed about. Then write these situations down. Also include in the list situations you have avoided as a strategy for preventing depression, as they indicate the presence of irrational beliefs. Maxine wrote the following list:

- my disappointing A-level results;
- my family asking me to carry on with my studies;
- watching TV hospital dramas;
- when my friends talk about going to university;
- when I think about my plans to go to Cambridge;
- when I think about my plans to be a doctor;
- when people ask me what my results were.

Step 2: Identify common inference themes

To look for common themes, first consider those situations where you were/are depressed, then think about recurring inference themes. For example, what Maxine's situations have in common is her perceived failure to reach those goals. So, as a general rule, she has problems with depression in situations where she infers that she has failed. Another way of identifying common themes is to consider whether the ABC assessments of your emotional problems are variations on a theme, for example being disapproved of or hardship.

In Chapter 2 we discussed some theories about psychological vulnerabilities to depression. As these theories concern common events and inferences that people depress themselves about, they can be helpful when you identify common situations and inference themes.

As we saw in Chapter 2, in 1983 Aaron T. Beck and some of his colleagues at the University of Pennsylvania grouped inferences in terms of the kind of events that are likely to precipitate depression. They identified two dimensions: autonomy and sociotropy.

Autonomy

This applies to those individuals who value (and demand) such autonomous characteristics as success, freedom and independence. When they are faced with events where they infer that success, freedom and independence are compromised they are likely to activate irrational beliefs, such as:

- *I must not fail; if I do then I'm a failure.*
- *I must not rely on others.*
- *I must not be depressed.*
- *I must maintain my status.*

Brian's common inference themes were about losing his useful role, losing his status and relying on others. These inference themes indicate an autonomy-type vulnerability to depression.

Sociotropy

The second dimension refers to a person's investment in relationships with other people. Such individuals tend to value (and demand) acceptance from others, support from others, and intimacy. As such they tend to activate irrational beliefs when they infer they are rejected, unsupported and unloved. Likely irrational beliefs for those who have sociotropic tendencies are:

- *I must be loved in my close relationships; if I'm not loved then I'm unlovable.*

- *I have to be approved of at all times by all people.*
- *I have to be looked after and supported by other people. I could not bear it if people withdrew their care and support for me.*

When Chris reviewed his recurrent inferences they were exclusively about sociotropic issues such as being loved and being looked after. By identifying these similarities in the inferences and events that trigger his irrational beliefs and depression, he was able to address these common or core beliefs directly, thus reducing the chance of depression should he be faced with the same event in the future.

Step 3: Identify your core depression-related irrational beliefs

When you have identified the recurrent themes of events and inferences that you disturb yourself about, you are in a position to find your core irrational beliefs. These beliefs are general in that the irrational belief underpins a number of different activating events. In Maxine's case, her recurrent inference was *I have failed* and her core irrational belief was *I must not fail and if I fail then I am a failure.* This influences a number of different areas in her life. If left unchallenged this irrational belief will continue to result in depression and other emotional problems when she is faced with inferred or actual incidents of failure.

As we discussed in Chapter 2, Dr Paul Hauck noticed that his depressed patients tended to have three different styles of depressing themselves with their irrational beliefs:

1 *Self-blame*	This was the first and most common form of irrationality and refers to the use of demanding beliefs with self-deprecation beliefs. Maxine engages in self-blame because (a) she demands she must not fail; and (b) she is self-deprecating in concluding that she is a failure.
2 *Self-pity*	This was the next most common form of irrationality associated with depression. Self-pity is the tendency to disturb yourself when you infer life is unfair or

87

that others have been unfair. This process of disturbing oneself generally involves demanding beliefs and awfulizing beliefs. Lily is engaging in self-pity, as her recurring inference is about unfairness and her beliefs are that *Life absolutely should be fair* and that *It is terrible that life is unfair.*

3 *Other pity*   This is the least common of the three types of irrationality and occurs when the inference is about the unfortunate experience of others, rather than yourself. Other pity involves demanding beliefs and awfulizing beliefs. Neelam engaged in other pity when she inferred that people experienced misfortune when they didn't deserve it. Her irrational beliefs about this event were that *People absolutely should not experience misfortune when they don't deserve it* and *It is terrible that people experience misfortune when they don't deserve it.*

Step 4: Question your core irrational beliefs

At this stage you can use the same process of challenging your specific irrational beliefs as described in Chapter 4. To demonstrate the challenging process with core beliefs let us revisit Maxine, who identified one of her core beliefs as *I must not fail. If I fail then that means I am a failure.*

As you can see from this belief, Maxine's core irrational belief involves the primary demanding belief and one of the derivatives, namely the self-depreciation beliefs. Let us remind you of the three major arguments with irrational beliefs:

- Is this belief true?
- Is this belief logical?
- Is this belief helpful?

Maxine asked herself the above questions about her irrational core demand and self-depreciating belief.

88

- *It is not true to say that I must not fail as there is no universal law that prevents me from doing so. If there were such a law I would never be able to fail anything ever! Sure, I don't want to fail, but I cannot logically conclude that I must not. To say I don't want to is flexible while to conclude I must not is inflexible, and you cannot logically derive an inflexible conclusion from a flexible starting point. Telling myself that I must not fail adds additional pressure and in fact has resulted in my not wanting to try anything where there is the risk of failure, so it is not a helpful belief.*
- *My belief that I am a failure is not true. I know this because if I were a failure then everything I have done would have failed. And I have plenty of evidence to the contrary. This belief is also illogical because I can realistically say that, as I'm human, there are some things I have failed at. But I can't logically write myself off as a failure on the basis of a few things. Telling myself I'm a failure yields unhealthy results; it means I'm less likely to try any new challenges and results in my feeling depressed, so as a belief it is unhelpful.*

You can use the three major arguments to question any irrational core beliefs you hold. If you identified with the styles of irrationality Hauck observed in his practice then here are some additional points to consider.

Self-blame

1 Self-blame does not alter your behaviour for the better, and the result is likely to be depression and dysfunctional behaviours.
2 Refraining from self-blame is not the same as refusing to take responsibility. You can still accept that you are responsible for your actions without damning yourself totally.
3 Rather than attributing a personal wrongdoing to being, for instance, bad or useless, you can attribute the wrongdoing to (a) stupidity on that occasion; (b) ignorance on that occasion; (c) emotional disturbance on that occasion.
4 If you self-blame then you are inconsistent because you can extend forgiveness to others but condemn yourself for the same behaviour.

89

Self-pity

1 By engaging in self-pity you rate your negative circumstances as 101 per cent when nothing can be more than 100 per cent bad.
2 It is unlikely that the circumstance is 100 per cent bad as unfortunately circumstances can get worse.
3 Believing that your circumstance is awful makes a bad situation worse.

Other pity

1 Telling yourself that others' misfortune is terrible brings additional needless worry to the world.
2 By depressing yourself you compromise your own ability to become an effective problem-solver.
3 By awfulizing about the plight of others you turn yourself into a poor role model, which may make the situation worse.

Step 5: Develop core rational beliefs

In this step you need to consider the core irrational belief and develop a core rational belief alternative. If, for example, your core irrational belief is, like Maxine's, *I must not fail and if I fail then that means I'm a failure*, then your rational belief would sound something like: *I very much prefer to succeed, but I do not always have to. If I fail I am not a failure but a fallible human being who can succeed and fail. As such I can learn from failure.*

Once you have developed your core rational belief, question the belief using the three major arguments you used with the irrational core belief (see Chapter 4 for guidance).

Step 6: Deepen your conviction regarding a core rational belief

The next step is to deepen your conviction in regard to your core rational belief. You do this in the same way as you deepen your conviction regarding a rational core belief about specific problems. First, you may wish to use the zigzag attack–response method described in Chapter 5. The difference between using these techniques with specific rational beliefs and rational core beliefs is that you will be addressing more general problems. Second, you need to act on your core rational beliefs. This is essential: without acting on your rational core beliefs you are unlikely to overcome them. Maxine initially used the REI technique and imagined herself returning to her studies while changing her irrational core belief to her new core rational belief. She then acted on her core rational belief by returning to school to restart her studies and making a note of the lessons she had learnt from her disappointing results.

Step 7: Reconsider general inferences and thinking consequences

In Chapter 6 we asked you to reconsider the inferences that you held at point A and C of your specific ABC: namely, reconsider the inference that served as your activating event and the thinking consequences of depression that can serve as future activating events. The same is true for reconsidering general depression-relating inferences and thinking consequences. To help you with this, refer to the questions in Chapter 6.

Once Maxine had challenged her irrational core belief and developed a rational core belief she reconsidered her general inference, *I failed.* As she had addressed her core irrational beliefs that determined her depression and reached her goal of healthy sadness, she was able to reconsider her inference without the distorting influence of depressed thinking consequences. In light of this she could see that her inference was not true: she had not done as well as she wanted but she had not failed.

Using setbacks

Ideally, the path from unhealthy depression to healthy sadness is smooth, but in reality it is likely that you will experience setbacks. Setbacks are opportunities for you to put into practice what you have learnt. How you react to a setback can be the difference between a lapse (going back a few steps) and a relapse (going back to where you started). If you identify the reasons for the lapse and learn from them you are less likely to experience future lapses. If, however, you do not learn from the lapse and disturb yourself about it you are more likely to turn this into a relapse.

For example, you may notice yourself reverting to depressed behaviour. If this is the case it is likely that you are reverting to the irrational beliefs that underpin the depression. You can deal with this by focusing on changing the behaviours as described in Chapter 3. In addition to this you will need to challenge and change the irrational beliefs that underpin the depression and behaviour consequences using the techniques in Chapter 4.

Emotional problems about depression can also be a common form of lapse: for example, shame about depression. If you have a second-order problem that is interfering with your progress then review the material in Chapter 7. In some cases you need to overcome the second-order problem before the primary problem of depression.

Low frustration tolerance beliefs about the change process of overcoming your depression can promote lapses and relapses. For example, you may find yourself saying that the change is too difficult and that you can't handle it. If this is the case you need to challenge your irrational beliefs, as in Chapter 4, so you can show yourself that change is difficult but that it is tolerable and worth tolerating in order to reach your goal of healthy sadness.

Finally, if you do not address the reasons for the lapse and if you demand that you must not experience lapses you are more likely to experience a relapse. In this case you need to challenge your irrational beliefs about the lapse and show yourself:

1 I don't want setbacks in my progress but I am not immune from setbacks and can learn from them.
2 Setbacks are bad but they are not awful and believing they are awful only makes a bad situation worse.
3 It is difficult to tolerate setbacks but I can tolerate them, and they are worth tolerating because I can learn from them and reduce the chances of them recurring.
4 Setbacks do not mean that I am weak or useless, but are evidence that I'm a fallible human being who can experience setbacks and progress in my goal to overcome my depression.

Contingency plans

Though ideally you will not disturb yourself in the future, there is no universal law preventing you from doing so. Through identifying your common inferences and core irrational beliefs you can identify where your vulnerabilities are. As a self-help strategy you can put together a contingency plan that you can refer to should you disturb yourself in the future. To form this plan, first refer to the general inferences and core beliefs you identified as a guide to those situations where you are more vulnerable to disturbing yourself. Second, make up a first-aid kit of the difficulties you faced while depressed, e.g. your likely behaviours or irrational beliefs, and the techniques that you used successfully to overcome these problems. Finally, keep a copy of this plan somewhere readily available to you, and if appropriate tell a spouse or good friend where it is so you can access it quickly if needed.

Summary

The strategies in this chapter are designed to help you prevent future episodes of depression and deal with setbacks. As we have discussed, setbacks are likely during the process of overcoming depression and can provide an excellent opportunity to put into practice what you have learnt. However, if you are not having any success with these self-help strategies you may need to consult your GP for advice.

This chapter has been about strategies for preventing future episodes of depression and how to deal with setbacks. In the next chapter we will bring together the steps from this book to help you overcome your depression and adopt an anti-depressant philosophy.

9

Prescriptions for an Anti-Depressant Philosophy

Introduction

In the previous chapter we showed you how you can limit the chances of future depression and how to deal with setbacks. In this chapter we will bring together the main points from this book to summarize the process of using Rational Emotive Behaviour Therapy to overcome depression step by step. We will conclude by returning to the 18 events and irrational core beliefs that underpin depression that we showed you in Chapter 2, and outline our prescription for an anti-depressant philosophy.

Sixteen steps to overcome depression

The following 16 steps review the stages of overcoming depression using the Rational Emotive Behaviour Therapy that we have discussed in this book. Listed with each step is the chapter where you will find details of how to go about the steps:

Step 1   Identify unhealthy depression as the problem and healthy sadness as the goal (Chapters 1 and 2).

Step 2   Assess an ABC about a specific problem (Chapter 2).

Step 3   Deal with depressed behaviour (Chapter 3).

Step 4   Challenge your specific irrational beliefs (Chapter 4).

Step 5   Develop rational beliefs (Chapter 4).

Step 6   Increase your conviction in rational beliefs (Chapter 5).

Step 7   Act on your rational beliefs (Chapter 5).

Step 8   Reconsider the inferences at point A and C in the ABC framework (Chapter 6).

Step 9   Deal with emotional problems about depression (Chapter 7).

Step 10   Repeat 1–9 for other specific depression problems (Chapters 1–7).

Step 11   Identify common inference themes and irrational core beliefs (Chapter 8).

Step 12   Challenge core irrational beliefs (Chapter 8).
Step 13   Develop core rational beliefs (Chapter 8).
Step 14   Act on your core rational beliefs (Chapter 8).
Step 15   Learn from setbacks (Chapter 8).
Step 16   Develop a contingency plan (Chapter 8).

The above steps are particularly useful when your depression is a reaction to situations and is mild or moderate, as this sort of depression tends to respond to self-help strategies. Remember that the more you practise, the better you will get at using these techniques to overcome your depression and the closer you will be to adopting an anti-depressant philosophy on life.

Prescriptions for an anti-depressant philosophy

As we have discussed many times through the course of this book, reactive depression is largely (but not exclusively) the result of irrational beliefs about an activating event. In our practice we have worked with many people with depression and helped them to reach a rational solution to their problem through the strategies detailed in this book. The majority of people have presented with irrational beliefs about the 18 areas described at the end of Chapter 2. What follow are our prescriptions concerning how to avoid being depressed in these 18 areas. Each prescription is based on a rational belief.

Failure

I very much prefer to succeed, but I do not always have to. If I fail I am not a failure, but a fallible human being who can succeed and fail. As such I can learn from failure.

Incompetence

I prefer to do well, but I do not always have to. If I do not do well then I am not an incompetent person but a fallible human being, who may not be doing well because the task is new to me or I do not have the talent to do so well without extra effort. I am a person who has a variety of talents and a variety of things I do not have talent for.

Loss of useful role

I very much prefer to be of use, but I do not always have to be useful. My worth is not dependent on being useful and there are other aspects of life, which are important. If I have lost a useful role, it does not mean I cannot be useful in other ways.

Loss of status

My status that I have lost is important to me but it is not the be-all and end-all of my life. My worth is not dependent on my status. There are other aspects of being a person, and while I very much miss my status I can involve myself in other aspects of life.

Relying on others

I value being self-sufficient and much prefer to be so, but I do not always have to be self-reliant. I am not a weak person if I have to rely on others. I am a person with strengths and weaknesses, and maybe it is a strength that I can be flexible enough to take help from others rather than a weakness. My worth is not defined by being self-sufficient.

Depression

I prefer not to be depressed but I am not immune from depression. Nobody is. Even if depression is a 'weakness' it does not mean that I am a weak person. It means that I am a fallible human being with strengths and weaknesses. Thus, I can admit my feelings and seek appropriate help.

Disapproval

I would like to be approved of, but do not always have to be. Being disapproved of may be more about the other person who is disapproving of me or it may mean that I have behaved poorly or have an unlikeable trait. If the latter is true it means that I am a fallible human being with likeable and unlikeable aspects and that I can accept myself as such and address what needs to be changed.

Loss of love

In close relationships, expressions of love may wax and wane and I do not always have to be loved. Even if the worst comes to the worst and somebody I love stops loving me, this is very sad but I am not immune from this. Losing love does not mean that I am unlovable. If it is true that the other person has stopped loving me because of an unlovable trait, I can always accept myself as a fallible human being with lovable and unlovable traits and resolve to maximize the former and address and change the latter if these can be changed.

Criticism

I would like not to be criticized but that does not mean I must not be criticized. When I am criticized it may mean more about the critic or more about me. However, if the latter is the case it does not mean that there is something wrong with me as a person, although it may mean that I need to do something about what is being criticized. In this case, accepting myself as a fallible human being with a myriad of good, bad and neutral aspects will help me to do this effectively.

Not belonging

I very much value being part of a social group but do not always need to belong. My worth is not dependent on belonging. I can accept myself as a fallible human being who is happier being part of a social group and thus make sensible attempts to rejoin this group or non-desperate attempts to join another. Moreover, I can still be happy (although not as happy) during times when I do not belong.

Loss of helping role

I like to help others, but I do not need to do this. A healthier balance to my life can be achieved when I help myself as well as others. My worth is not dependent on helping others; thus I do not have to seek out others to help.

Unattractiveness

I would like to be more attractive than I am, but I do not have to be. I am not an ugly person but a person who has attractive and unattractive features. Even if I am not as attractive as I would like to be, I am attractive to some people even though I find this hard to acknowledge.

Others withdrawing care and support

While I might prefer to be looked after, I do not need to be, and if I seek out others to help me rather than helping myself, I may be comfortable in the short term but remain vulnerable in the long term. Even though it is difficult, uncomfortable and unfamiliar, I can work towards being more resourceful as a person.

Unfairness to self

It would be great if life could be fair to me when I deserve it, but unfortunately it doesn't have to be. Sadly, there is no one-to-one correspondence between what I deserve and what I get. So it is in the interests of my mental health if I accept that it is not terrible to be treated unfairly and that life is a complex mixture of the fair and unfair.

Others' misfortune

It would be great if life was not cruel in allowing others to experience misfortune when they do not deserve it, but sadly life does not have to be the way I would like it. Life is not terrible for allowing such misfortunes to exist since it is a complex mixture of the fortunate and unfortunate. This philosophy will encourage me to help others when it is appropriate and when I am able to do those things which I could not do if I was depressed.

Hardship

Life is hard at the moment, but sadly it does not have to be easier than it is. So let me see what I have that is valuable if things cannot be changed at present.

Bereavement

I certainly would clearly want my loved one to be here, but tragically there is no law of the universe which states that s/he absolutely should not have died. My life has been deeply affected by the loss but it has not lost all meaning, and life is still worth living even though at times I may think that it is not.

Goal frustration

I would like to achieve my goal easily, but unfortunately there is no law of nature that decrees that I must do so. Frustration is just that, frustrating, but it is tolerable and I can tolerate struggling to achieve my goal. I can persist at overcoming obstacles towards my goals, and if at the end of the day I am unable to overcome them, this is very unfortunate but hardly terrible and I can choose to pursue other goals.

Summary

Through using the self-help strategies in this book we hope that you will develop an anti-depressant philosophy. In the final chapter we will revisit the seven people we have used as examples to demonstrate how they applied REBT to depression and associated problems to reach an anti-depressant philosophy.

10

How Seven People Overcame Depression

Introduction

In this final chapter we will return to the seven people whom we have discussed throughout this book in the case studies to show how they used Rational Emotive Behaviour Therapy to overcome depression, in their own particular ways, by replacing it in each case with a sense of sadness.

Maxine

We have used Maxine to illustrate many points throughout this book. As you may recall, she felt depressed about her mock A-level results and her depression was partly related to her inference that the drop in results was a sign of failure. However, central to her depression was her irrational belief, *I have to achieve perfect results in my A-level exams.* A thinking consequence of her depression was to tell herself that because she had not done perfectly well (as she should have done) she had failed. This thinking consequence triggered her irrational belief that *I must succeed at all things I attempt; if I were to fail then this would prove that I am a failure.*

As well as feeling the unhealthy negative emotion of depression Maxine stopped her studies and resolved to avoid ever risking failure again. By doing this she denied herself the chance to improve on her grade or, more importantly, develop the ability to cope with and learn from perceived failure. As a result of her depression she also thought about other occasions when she had not achieved what she wanted. She focused on these events to the point where she only considered past 'failings'.

Unfortunately Maxine also disturbed herself about feeling depressed: she demanded that she must pull herself together and stop feeling depressed, and concluded that she was a weak person. As a consequence she was unhealthily angry. Sometimes she would hurt herself by hitting the wall until her hands bled. So when we met

Maxine at the start of the book her belief that she must never fail was having an extreme impact on her life.

By using Rational Emotive Behaviour Therapy Maxine addressed her depression about her A-level results. She was able to show herself that her irrational belief was untrue, illogical and unhelpful and that instead she could create rational beliefs for herself that, if she were to really believe them, would help determine a healthy negative emotion of sadness. This would in turn help her to look at the positive and negative aspects of her A-level results. She developed a rational belief that:

> *I really want to achieve perfect results in my A levels but there is no law that states that I must do so. Not doing perfectly wouldn't mean that I am a failure but rather a fallible human being who on this occasion did not achieve the grades I desire.*

In order to believe her alternative rational belief Maxine put it to the test, first by using the same rigorous questions she used to test her irrational beliefs, namely: is my belief true, logical and helpful? Second, she worked hard to integrate her rational belief by using rational emotive imagery. She then acted on her healthy belief by making an appointment with her teacher to discuss her results and review her revision strategy.

Once she had successfully disputed her rational beliefs and integrated them into her belief system she returned to her depression-derived inference that she would always fail. She showed herself that the inference was inaccurate, as there is no way of knowing whether she would always fail. In fact, her previous performance would suggest that she was more (though not always) likely to succeed.

Maxine also looked at her initial inference that she had not achieved perfect results and questioned whether she could view this differently. As a consequence she concluded that she had not done *perfectly* but she had done well. Maxine was able to reconsider her inferences with good effect because her rational beliefs helped her to view the inference from a more objective frame of mind.

As we discussed, Maxine had a secondary emotional problem as she was angry about being depressed. This anger was a result of her irrational demand: *I must pull myself together and not be depressed. As I have not done so this means that I am a weak and pathetic person who can't get a grip.* She expressed her anger physically by hitting her hands against the wall.

Eventually she was able to dispute her irrational beliefs by developing and integrating the following rational belief into her belief system:

> *Although I would rather be able to stop feeling depressed I am not immune from depression. Telling myself I am weak and pathetic for my depression is not true. Even if my depression is a weakness, this does not make me a weak person. It means that I am a fallible human being with both strengths and weaknesses. Accepting this fact will help me take the necessary steps to overcome my depression and anger.*

By acting in accordance with her rational beliefs she was able to stop hurting herself and think constructively about how she could help herself overcome her depression.

In order to help prevent future episodes of depression Maxine identified those situations she had disturbed herself about and wrote down the inference themes. In her case the situations were when she perceived that she had failed to reach her ideal goal.

If you recall from Chapters 1 and 8, this inference suggests that Maxine may have an autonomy-type vulnerability to depression. She also identified the fact that when she disturbed herself as a general rule she engaged in what Dr Paul Hauck would term 'self-blame', i.e. her irrational beliefs were a combination of demands and self-depreciation (see Chapter 8). With these insights Maxine was able to identify and change her unhealthy core belief (*I have to succeed at all times*) to the following core rational belief:

> *I want to succeed at all times but I don't have to; if I am unsuccessful then this is proof that I'm a fallible human being who can succeed and fail. By acknowledging this fact I am more likely to learn from my mistakes and take constructive action.*

As such, Maxine is more accepting of herself and is less prone to depression.

102

Brian

Brian had two main problems: first, he was depressed as the date of his mandatory retirement drew closer, and second, he was ashamed about his depression. As a result of this shame, Brian began to avoid social situations, and when he was prescribed anti-depressants by his GP he kept this secret. As these two behavioural consequences significantly interfered with work he was doing to overcome his depression, it was appropriate for him to deal with his shame before continuing to work on his depression.

Using the ABC assessment detailed in Chapter 2, Brian identified that he was most ashamed about his inference that people would look down on him if they knew he was depressed. His ABC assessment of shame was:

A   Activating event = Others will look down on me if they know I'm depressed.

B   Irrational beliefs = Others must not look down on me; if they did, this would be terrible.

C   Emotional consequence = Shame.
       Behavioural consequence = Keeps the diagnosis from the GP secret and hides his prescription and avoids social situations.

By showing himself that his irrational beliefs were illogical, unhelpful and untrue Brian was able to construct and act on the following rational belief that promoted a healthy feeling of disappointment:

> *Although it would be nice to have a guarantee preventing others from looking down on me I do not have one. While it may be a negative experience if others were to look down on me I cannot conclude that it is terrible, as there are worse things that can happen to me. Besides, by telling myself that it would be terrible I create more emotional problems for myself.*

As Brian was disappointed rather than ashamed, he told his wife about his meeting with the GP and the prescription that he had been given. Rather than looking down on him Brian's wife was supportive. Brian later went on to question the inference that he held at point A and he concluded:

Some people may look down on me and some people won't. What is important is how I react to this problem, and avoiding social situations and not taking my medication is not going to help me overcome my depression.

By reaching this point Brian was in a much stronger position to address his depression. He went on to realize that, although he did not want to lose the useful role as a local bank manager, this was not the worst thing that could happen and was in no way an indication that he was totally useless. As a result he felt sad about this loss but was able to consider both the positive and negative aspects of his retirement and take constructive action by focusing his attention on developing other interests. He used the attack–response method detailed in Chapter 5 to help integrate rational beliefs into his belief system.

As a preventative strategy Brian identified the fact that he was more likely to depress himself when he faced situations where he inferred that he had lost status, usefulness or independence. So he was more likely to prevent future depressions by identifying the associated core belief: *I have to be useful at all times; if I am not useful I am useless and will never be of use again.* He showed himself why this core belief is unhelpful, illogical and untrue and instead developed the following more rational core belief:

I very much prefer to be of use, but I do not always have to be useful and there are other aspects of life which are important. If I have lost a useful role it does not mean that I cannot be useful in other ways.

As a result Brian has involved himself in fundraising for a local charity and has learnt to enjoy activities such as gardening and spending time with his family, activities that he would not have entertained when we first met him in Chapter 1.

Chris

Chris believed that he was an unlovable person. He traced this belief back to his childhood when his parents had left him in the care of his grandmother. From that point on he envied other people who had loving relationships. When he started to date someone with whom he worked, he was preoccupied with the idea that she would leave him for someone 'better', and when she grew tired of his insecurities and left him, he took this as further confirmation that he was unlovable. To protect himself he vowed never to risk rejection again. So he turned down invitations to socialize. After a while the invitations stopped and he took this as further confirmation that there was something wrong with him and that he was unlovable.

By assessing his ABC of depression about his girlfriend leaving he had identified (A) that he had lost the love of his girlfriend. He evaluated this irrationally at point (B) by saying that his girlfriend must love him and the withdrawal of love meant that he was an unlovable person. The consequence of holding these irrational beliefs was that he was depressed about the loss and, as we have already discussed, he kept himself to himself, fearing that he might experience future rejection if he were to enter into a relationship again.

By using REBT to challenge his irrational beliefs, Chris was able to show himself that even though he wanted his ex-girlfriend to love him (and demonstrate her love for him at all times) he could not logically conclude that she had to. He also showed himself that the belief that his partner must love him and demonstrate this love at all times was not in fact consistent with reality as she had left him. Most importantly, Chris was able to challenge his irrational belief and concluded that even if his girlfriend stopped loving him this did not mean that he was a totally unlovable person, but rather that this particular person did not love him. Questioning the specific irrational beliefs and creating rational beliefs helped him mourn the loss of his girlfriend, while also seeing that there was hope for the future. Because Chris was now healthily sad about the loss of the relationship and no longer believed himself to be unlovable, he went on to take some risks by accepting social invitations.

While reviewing other situations where he had experienced

depression Chris noticed there were similarities in the inferences that triggered his irrational beliefs. He realized that he had a sociotropic vulnerability to depression. If you recall from Chapter 2 and Chapter 8, sociotropic inferences are those inferences concerned with relationship issues such as intimacy, sharing and affection. Chris also identified the fact that he was particularly depression-prone when, after someone he loved had stopped loving him in return, he inferred that he had a demand that he must not lose the love of someone he loved. He identified his core irrational belief as *I must not lose the love of those people I love*. Through showing himself that this belief was illogical, unhelpful and untrue, Chris developed a core rational belief:

> *In close relationships love may wax and wane and I don't always have to be loved. Even if the worst comes to the worst and somebody I love stops loving me, this is very sad but I am not immune from it. Losing love does not mean I am unlovable. If it is true that the other person has stopped loving me because of an unlovable trait, I can always accept myself as a fallible human being with lovable and unlovable traits and resolve to maximize the former and address and change the latter if these can be changed.*

Chris is now more able to seek out and maintain healthy relationships or even to remain single without regarding this as an untenable situation (i.e. without 'awfulizing' his circumstances).

Neelam

As you may remember from Chapter 1, Neelam took a keen interest in the welfare of others and started to work in the soup kitchen of a homeless shelter. Rather than seeing the contribution she was making, she considered her efforts to be insignificant. She focused on the plight of the homeless people she worked with and before long she started to feel depressed about others' misfortune. She depressed herself when she inferred at point A that other people experience misfortune which they do not deserve. At point B of the

ABC of her depression, she demanded that *People should not experience misfortune when they do not deserve it. If they do this is terrible and the world is a cruel place.* Her depressed thinking consequences resulted in her only seeing pain and darkness in the future, and with this in mind she stopped going to the soup kitchen to help. As her depression continued she felt less motivated and attempted to eliminate her feelings of depression by drinking alcohol.

The irrational beliefs that underpinned and largely determined her depression were similar in content to 'other pity' beliefs, the type of depression promoting irrational beliefs first described by Dr Paul Hauck. As such there were a number of points that Neelam could use to argue against her irrational other pity. First, by telling herself that other people's misfortune is terrible she actually brings additional needless worry to the world. Second, by depressing herself about other people's misfortune she compromises her own ability to become an effective helper. Finally, by awfulizing about the plight of others, Neelam turns herself into a poor role model, which may make the situation worse. If Neelam were to challenge her irrational beliefs by asking 'Is this belief true?', 'Is this belief sensible?', 'Is this belief helpful to my psychological well-being?' and proving to herself that the answer was 'no', she would have constructed the following belief:

It would be great if the world was not cruel in allowing others to experience misfortune when they don't deserve it but sadly life does not have to be the way I would like it. Life is not terrible for allowing such misfortunes to exist since it is a complex mixture of the fortunate and unfortunate. This philosophy will encourage me to help others when it is appropriate and when I am able, something I could not do if I were depressed.

Armed with this new rational belief, Neelam will feel healthily sad about the plight of those people she worked with at the homeless shelter. As such she is more likely to have thinking consequences that enable her to look to the future with some hope. As she is healthily sad rather than unhealthily depressed, she will have no need to eliminate her feelings of pain with alcohol and will regain her motivation. As such she is more likely to continue her work at the soup kitchen and, importantly, to see her efforts as significant to those she helps.

Sylvia

We met Sylvia in Chapter 1 and again in Chapter 3, when we showed you how you can help yourself overcome depression by changing self-defeating behaviours such as inactivity. Sylvia disturbed herself when the last of her children left home. When she felt depressed she stayed at home on her own and spent her time reminiscing about the past. When she thought about the future she thought she would be of no help to anyone. As her mood deteriorated she had less and less energy; she responded to this by doing less and less, and the less she did the less she felt like doing. Eventually Sylvia had lost her motivation to the point where making a cup of tea or washing her hair was an enormous effort.

Through her inactivity Sylvia had provided herself with hours of dedicated time to think about how she had lost her family and her role within the family; she focused almost entirely on her self-deprecating belief that she was useless. Her lack of motivation and inactivity meant that she denied herself the chance to demonstrate that she could in fact help herself. As such she reinforced the thinking consequence that she was helpless.

In order to overcome her depression Sylvia started to identify and change those behaviours that were self-defeating. This was particularly important for Sylvia as the process helped her to gather current evidence that she was able to help herself and was by no means totally useless. She used the activity scheduling method detailed in Chapter 3. By assessing her behaviour and mood fluctuations for a typical day (while depressed) she identified times of the day when her mood was at its worst (early mornings) and she also noticed that periods of inactivity could influence her mood, and vice versa.

Sylvia set about scheduling activities into her day and, importantly, these were activities she would ordinarily enjoy or from which she would gain a sense of achievement and were tailored to account for the variation in her mood throughout the day (i.e. easier activities when her mood was worst in the mornings). She carried out her schedule and realized that maintaining some activity in her day, even though she initially didn't feel like it, helped improve her motivation. This process also provided Sylvia with evidence that she was not totally useless, which was helpful when she went on to dispute her irrational beliefs.

Sylvia's depression started when the last of her children left home and she inferred that she had lost her helping role within the family. Sylvia's depression about losing this helping role was based on the irrational demand: *I have to be helpful to my family. Because the last of my children has left home and my husband is away working, I am not helpful to my family and thus I have no worth.* If Sylvia had challenged her irrational belief she could have helped herself to develop the following rational belief:

> *I wish that I still had my helping role within the family but I do not need to be helpful. A healthier balance to my life can be achieved when I help myself as well as my family. My worth is not dependent on whether I am helping my family.*

If Sylvia were to believe this rational belief she would feel sad about losing her helping role in the family, and as such she would be able to see both the negative and positive aspects of her son leaving and would be able to look to the future with hope.

Sylvia would then have been motivated to address her more general irrational belief: *I have to be helpful to others; if I am not helpful then I have no worth.* By challenging her general irrational belief Sylvia would first assume her inference that she was not helping others. She would then go on to prove to herself that: *There is no law of the universe that states that I have to be helpful to others even though I would want to be helpful rather than unhelpful.* And so she developed the following core rational belief:

> *I like to help others, but I do not need to do this. A healthier balance to my life can be achieved when I help myself as well as others. My worth is not dependent on helping others; thus I do not need to seek out others to help.*

Armed with this core rational belief, Sylvia would be less likely to experience depression whenever she inferred that she was not helpful, and more likely to develop interests for herself that did not involve being helpful to others.

Lily

Lily experienced depression when, despite her efforts, she discovered that she was not as skilled as the other dancers at the ballet school and had not been chosen to dance one of the main parts in the production. Lily's feeling of depression stemmed from the following irrational belief: *Because I worked hard to improve my ballet technique I absolutely should have been treated fairly and deserve a bigger part in the production. This unfairness is terrible and I can't tolerate it.*

Lily disturbed herself by concluding that her dance teacher had been unfair in not choosing her and that it was terrible that she had been unfairly treated.

Dr Paul Hauck described the process of disturbing oneself by demanding, awfulizing and low frustration tolerance beliefs as 'self-pity'. So she could have challenged her irrational beliefs by showing herself that by engaging in self-pity she rates not being treated fairly as terrible, i.e. more than 100 per cent bad, and nothing can be more than 100 per cent bad. In addition, it is unlikely that not being treated fairly is over 100 per cent bad, as unfortunately the situation could get worse. Finally, by believing that the situation could not get any worse, Lily in fact made the situation worse and, as a result, increased her depression.

In order to overcome her depression about being treated unfairly as well as challenging her irrational beliefs, she would also need to develop and internalize rational beliefs about being treated unfairly. As such Lily could have developed the rational belief:

It would be great if I had been treated fairly and given a larger part in the production, particularly as I worked so hard to improve my technique, but unfortunately I don't have to be given a larger part. Sadly there is no one-to-one correspondence

110

*between what I deserve and what I get. So it is in the interests of
my mental health and my future career as a dancer to accept that
it is not terrible to be treated unfairly and that life is a complex
mixture of the fair and unfair.*

As a result of changing her irrational beliefs to rational beliefs Lily
would feel sad about not being treated fairly and would be able to
reassess this inference without the contaminating effect of depression. When she considered whether there might be an alternative
reason for her not having been chosen for a larger part, she
concluded that there might have been a different, and possibly fair,
reason. She could easily test out this theory by asking for some
feedback from her dance teacher.

Colin

Colin was the last case example we showed you in Chapter 1. He
had been depressed on a number of previous occasions and each
time he deteriorated into a severe depression. When Colin started to
feel the familiar symptoms of depression he reacted by avoiding any
sort of activity: he stopped washing, didn't shave and stopped his
morning walk to buy the paper, so he didn't read. He couldn't be
bothered to cook so he ate less, and because he slept badly at night
he slept during the day.

Colin deteriorated quickly because he lacked motivation and
energy, but in addition to this he inferred that he was unable to
influence any symptoms of his depression and this included his low
motivation. Because he demanded that he must control and eradicate
his depression and he had not done so, he concluded that he was a
weak man, incapable of helping himself. This in turn reinforced his
inference that he was unable to influence his depression so there was
no point in his trying.

With the help of a psychologist Colin started to act against his
depression-derived thinking that he was helpless by introducing
some activity into his day. Once he had gained some success with
influencing his behaviour, he shifted his attention to addressing his
irrational beliefs that underpinned his depression about being

111

depressed. He identified his irrational belief as: *I must not be depressed. Depression is a sign of weakness. If I am depressed then I am weak.* His psychologist helped him to challenge his irrational beliefs about his depression and develop and integrate the following rational and healthy belief about depression:

> *I prefer not to be depressed but I am not immune from depression. Nobody is. Even if my depression is a 'weakness' it does not mean that I am a weak person. It means that I am a fallible human being with strengths and weaknesses. Thus I can admit my feelings and seek appropriate help.*

By being accepting of himself and realistically viewing himself as a man with both strengths and weaknesses, he was in a stronger position to help himself, which he did. When Colin had eventually worked through his depression with the help of relevant professionals, he wrote a plan for himself should he feel depressed in the future. In this plan he wrote down all the behaviours and irrational beliefs he had experienced and the techniques he had used to overcome them. He kept a copy of this plan should he need it in the future.

A final word

We have now reached the end of this book. We hope that, by adopting the techniques of Rational Emotive Behaviour Therapy as outlined above, you will learn a set of useful strategies to help you overcome your depression and instead feel a sense of healthy sadness – and thus develop an anti-depressant approach that will fortify you in dealing with life's problems.

Index

113